Better Homes and Gardens®

CHRISTMAS
sweets & treats

Meredith® Books
Des Moines, Iowa

Better Homes and Gardens® Christmas Sweets & Treats

Editor: Carrie E. Holcomb
Contributing Editors: Susan M. Banker, Ellen Boeke
Contributing Photo Editor: Staci Bailey
Contributing Designer: Studio P2, Craig Hanken
Copy Chief: Terri Fredrickson
Publishing Operations Manager: Karen Schirm
Senior Editor, Asset and Information Manager: Phillip Morgan
Edit and Design Production Coordinator: Mary Lee Gavin
Editorial Assistant: Cheryl Eckert
Book Production Managers: Pam Kvitne,
    Marjorie J. Schenkelberg, Rick von Holdt, Mark Weaver
Contributing Copyeditor: Judy Friedman
Contributing Proofreaders: Callie Dunbar, Karen Fraley, Jody Speer
Indexer: Elizabeth Parson
Test Kitchen Director: Lynn Blanchard
Test Kitchen Product Supervisor: Marilyn Cornelius
Test Kitchen Home Economists: Juliana Hale, Laura Harms, R.D.,
    Jennifer Kalinowski, R.D., Maryellyn Krantz, Jill Moberly, Dianna Nolin,
    Colleen Weeden, Lori Wilson, Charles Worthington

Meredith® Books
Executive Director, Editorial: Gregory H. Kayko
Executive Director, Design: Matt Strelecki
Senior Editor/Group Manager: Jan Miller

Publisher and Editor in Chief: James D. Blume
Editorial Director: Linda Raglan Cunningham
Executive Director, New Business Development: Todd M. Davis
Executive Director, Sales: Ken Zagor
Director, Operations: George A. Susral
Director, Production: Douglas M. Johnston
Director, Marketing: Amy Nichols
Business Director: Jim Leonard

Vice President and General Manager: Douglas J. Guendel

Meredith Publishing Group
President: Jack Griffin
Vice President: Bob Mate

Meredith Corporation
Chairman and Chief Executive Officer: William T. Kerr
President and Chief Operating Officer: Stephen M. Lacy

In Memoriam: E.T. Meredith III (1933-2003)

Test Kitchen

Our seal assures you that every recipe in *Christmas Sweets & Treats* has been tested in the *Better Homes and Gardens*® Test Kitchen. This means that each recipe is practical and reliable, and meets our high standards of taste appeal. We guarantee your satisfaction with this book for as long as you own it.

Pictured on the cover:
Reindeer Cookies, page 40.

it's the merry little things...

When I think about my most memorable Christmases ... it isn't the store-bought things that come to mind. It's those special things that friends and family did for me.

I remember the lovingly handmade gifts I've received—whether it was a bright knit scarf or a fragile ornament made from a child's hands.

I remember the times visiting loved ones and being surrounded with glorious handcrafted decorations that magically filled the room with the spirit of the season.

I remember the homemade cookies and candies my neighbors and friends delivered. They made our kitchen the most favorite hangout in the house.

It's memories like these I treasure most.

Christmas Sweets and Treats helps you spread that same heartfelt joy to your family and friends. You'll be delighted with incredible holiday recipes like Smoked Salmon Mousse and Candy Cane Cookies. Decorating will be a cinch with step-by-step directions for beautiful garlands, wreaths, ornaments, and more—some easy enough for kids to make. And the gift ideas! Well, let's just say everyone's Christmas will be very merry and bright.

So get ready to make this Christmas sparkle—you'll be the one to thank for making longlasting memories for those you love.

Warm holiday wishes!
Pat Adrian

contents

all through the house

fireplace magic

Nontraditional holiday colors—golden brown and green—inspire this rich garland accented with a bushel full of fruit.

1. Cluster magnolia branches into groups of three, wiring together at the stems. Working at a slight angle, fit each cluster tightly into the previous cluster; wire to secure. Form garland to the desired length.

2. Attach fruit in clusters with wire or hyacinth sticks. To attach with wire, work wire through center of fruit, leaving extra wire to secure to garland. To attach with hyacinth sticks, skewer the fruit to the sticks. Place the fruit at different angles between the leaves on the garland; attach with wire.

3. Place small nails diagonally into the corners where the mantel meets the wall. Drape the garland over the mantel; hold it in place with the nails. Shape the garland.

supplies

Small magnolia branches

Medium-gauge floral wire

Wire cutter

60 assorted artificial pears

Hyacinth sticks (optional)

Small nails

Hammer

minty topiaries

Quick to make and dressed in holiday colors, mint candy trees look elegant displayed on silver candlestick holders.

supplies

Round peppermint candies, candy spearmint leaves, or candy canes in green and white or red and white

Plastic-foam cone

Hot-glue gun and glue sticks

Ornate silver candlestick holders

1. Unwrap the peppermint candies, candy spearmint leaves, or candy canes if necessary.

2. For the topiaries using round peppermints or spearmint leaves: Working in rows and starting at the base of the plastic-foam cone, glue a flat side of candy to the cone shape. Continue gluing candies on the cone until the surface of the cone is covered.

3. For the topiaries using candy canes: Glue the candy canes vertically on the cone with the crook of the candy cane facing outward at the bottom of the cone.

4. At the top of each cone, glue the edge of a peppermint candy to act as the star.

5. Set the candy topiary on top of a candlestick holder.

candy striper candles

These small scale beauties light up a table setting. To create the look, gather a clear-glass votive, a small candy cane, a sprig of holly, and sheer red ribbon. Tie a ribbon bow around the votive candleholder, then tuck in the candy cane and holly. Trim the ribbon ends. **Note**: Never leave burning candles unattended.

confetti ornaments

For festive sparkle hang fanciful ornaments on the Christmas tree or from the chandelier or windows.

supplies

Scissors; 9 yards of metallic braid in green, purple, blue, and gold

Embroidery needle (large enough to thread the braid yet small enough to go through beads)

Multicolor glass Rochaille "E" beads

Straight pins; paper; pencil; 1/3 yard clear plastic vinyl

Multicolored metallic confetti; tape

Sewing machine; metallic thread

Pinking shears or decorative-edge scissors; hole punch

1. Cut the braid into nine 1-yard lengths. Thread the needle with one braid and knot one end. Thread 8 to 10 inches with beads. Remove the needle, knot the other end of the braid, and push half of the beads toward each end. Repeat for the remaining eight braid lengths.

2. Pin together three beaded braids, keeping half of the beads at each end. Twist the braids together between the beaded ends. Knot just above the beads. Repeat for each group of three braids.

3. On paper draw a 4-inch-high star, heart, or diamond; cut out shapes.

4. Cut six 6-inch squares of vinyl. Place about 1 tablespoon of confetti in the center of one square. Place the second square of vinyl on top of the first, sandwiching the confetti; pin in place. Center a paper shape under the vinyl sandwich. Use tape to hold the paper in place.

5. Thread the sewing machine and bobbin with metallic thread. Place the sandwich, paper side down, under the presser foot. Using the pattern as a guide, stitch 1/4 inch in from the pattern edge through the vinyl and the paper. Cut around the pattern edges with pinking shears or decorative-edge scissors. Carefully tear paper away from stitching.

6. Punch a hole in the top and bottom of the ornament. Fold beaded braid in half. Thread it through the bottom hole and knot it 3 inches from the fold. Thread the folded end through the top hole for a hanger.

sprinkle ornaments

Blanket a round foam ball in glistening glass beads to reflect the holiday lights. To make these sparkling globes, thread a piece of heavy crafts wire through a white plastic-foam ball. Secure one end into the ball and twist the other for a hanger. Coat the foam ball with thick white crafts glue and sprinkle with tube-shape glass beads allowing some of the white foam to show through.

jeweled christmas balls

Dress ornaments in jewels to be the star attractions on the Christmas tree.

supplies

Solid-color round ornament

Juice glass; tweezers

Round jewels

Thick white crafts glue

Gold glitter paint pen

Soft cloth

Ball chain bracelet to match
   ornament top

Fresh or plastic sprigs of
   holiday greenery

1. Place an ornament on a juice glass to keep it from rolling while embellishing. Using tweezers, arrange the jewels on the top half of the ball, securing the jewels with glue. Let the glue dry.

2. Turn the ornament and continue adding jewels to achieve the desired look. Let dry.

3. Outline each jewel with glitter paint pen, carefully outlining the jewel shape. Gently wipe any glitter from the jewel using a soft cloth. Let the paint dry and repeat for the opposite side of the ornament.

4. Thread ball chain bracelet through the loop at the ornament top. Connect the clasp ends. Tuck a sprig of fresh or plastic greenery through the ornament loop.

polished pretty

Personalize a simple ornament with a decorative coat of color and design. To get the look, paint solid areas, swirls, and stripes of glitter or plain nail polish on the ornament and let dry.

tussie-mussies

Pretty bouquets add fresh-picked loveliness to evergreen branches.

1. For each tussie-mussie, fold over the ribbon end. Cover the plastic-foam cone by wrapping the ribbon around the cone, pinning to secure. To provide dimension, randomly fold the ribbon edges and bunch the ribbon to create softness. Pin the remaining ribbon end to the top of the cone.

2. Use a screwdriver to poke a starter hole in the center of the flat end of the cone.

3. Gently push the vial into the starter hole in the flat end of the cone. If it won't go in without using too much force, remove it and enlarge the hole using the screwdriver. Insert the vial into the hole. Fill the florist's vial with water. Place the flowers into the vial.

4. Pin additional bows and a hanging loop around the flowers.

supplies

1½ yards of 2-inch-wide wired-edge organdy ribbon

7- to 8-inch-long plastic-foam cones

Corsage pins

Screwdriver

2- to 3-inch-long florist's vials

Water

Small bouquets of dainty fresh flowers

shimmering centerpiece

Create a stunning tabletop by combining shimmery silver holiday decorations.

1. Wrap the taper candles together using nonflammable cording. Be careful to stop wrapping the candles near the top to avoid burning within one inch of the cord. Pin the ends to secure.

2. Secure the candle bottoms to the bowl bottom using a piece of candle gum on each candle.

3. Tuck silver tinsel around the base of the candles, filling the bowl to the top.

4. Arrange the bead garland and ball ornaments on the tinsel bed, allowing some of the garland to drape over the bowl edge. Place the bowl carefully onto the tray.

Note: Never leave burning candles unattended.

supplies

6 taper candles in white or silver

Nonflammable silver cord

Silver pins

Silver bowl

Candle gum

Silver tinsel

Silver bead garland

Silver ball ornaments

Silver tray

accessorized tabletop

Give holiday table settings an elegant, unexpected twist by putting your costume jewelry to work. Large bracelets make perfect napkin rings, and necklaces add panache to hurricane lamps. If a necklace is too short to drape around the lamp, use fine wire to extend it.

goblet centerpiece

Mismatched goblets come together beautifully to create a stunning centerpiece.

1. Fill the goblets with water.

2. Place a floating candle into each goblet and shake some confetti into the water.

3. Arrange the goblets on a tray, mantel, or table centerpiece. Light the candles for a glorious display.

Note: Never leave burning candles unattended.

Tip: To match your holiday color scheme, add a drop or two of food coloring into the water before adding the candles and confetti.

Tip: To help prevent accidental tipping of the goblets, weigh them down by placing clear glass marbles in the bottoms.

supplies

Clear glass goblets

Water

Floating white heart or star
  candles to fit goblets

Heart confetti

Food coloring (optional)

Marbles (optional)

artful arrangement

A large glass container lets you show off your finest ornaments while protecting them from damage. Fill a clear glass vase, compote, or snifter with pearly white and gold ornaments. Providing an all-around view, this ornament display is a visual treat as a centerpiece.

frosted ornament swag

Have a ball crafting a tight strand of ornaments for impact around a window.

supplies

1 set of metal curtain tiebacks

Medium-weight chain, available in
   hardware stores and home centers

Wire cutters

Hot-glue gun and glue
   sticks (optional)

Plastic or glass ball ornaments
   in desired color(s)

Silver-color wire

Newspapers

Matte finish spray

1. Place tiebacks just outside the window frame with the ends facing upward as shown in the photo.

2. Cut a length of chain long enough to drape between the tiebacks and hang down on each side. If desired, hot-glue the cap of each ornament to the ornament. Attach each ornament to the chain with narrow silver-color wire.

3. Group the balls by color or mix them randomly. Continue adding balls to the chain until full.

4. In a well-ventilated work area, cover the work surface with newspapers. Mist the garland with matte finish spray to give some balls a frosted look. Let dry.

5. Carefully hang the garland from the tiebacks.

light dressing

Swaddled in sheer fabric, white tree lights cast a soft glow to top off a window with holiday glee.

1. Determine the desired length of the fabric swag. Cut the fabric length to that measurement.

2. Loosely wrap white sheer fabric around white-corded clear miniature lights.

3. Install small hooks, nails, or drapery brackets at both upper corners of the window frame. Position the light-filled fabric between the hooks and arrange until the swag ends are even and the center hangs at the desired height.

4. Tie satin ribbon bows; using silver picks or garland, tuck bows into each corner of the window treatment. Trim the ribbon ends.

supplies

White fabric, such as cheesecloth, tulle, or drapery sheer

Scissors

White-corded clear miniature cool-burning lights

Small hooks, nails, or drapery brackets

Hammer and or screwdriver

Satin ribbon in desired colors

Scissors

Silver holiday picks or garland

festive finds

Showcase favorite ornaments and toppers by arranging them in a vintage pedestal bowl resting on an ornate tray.

1. In a well-ventilated work area, cover the work surface with newspapers. Spray-paint the holly silver. Let the paint dry. Turn the leaves over and spray-paint the backs. Let dry.

2. Place the pedestal bowl onto the tray.

3. Fill the bowl with tinsel garland to act as a cushion for the toppers. Arrange the toppers in the bowl, pointing the tips in different directions.

4. Tuck silver holly leaves and ball ornaments in and around the bowl and next to the tray.

supplies

Newspapers

Artificial holly leaves

Silver spray paint

Clear pedestal bowl

Ornate silver tray

Tinsel garland

Colorful Christmas tree toppers

Colorful glass ball ornaments

topper parade

Christmas tree toppers stand at attention beautifully on a mantel or shelf. To be sure they don't topple, use poster putty to hold them in place. Surround the bases with fresh or artificial greenery for a lovely accent that takes just a minute or two to arrange.

fruity pursuit

Create a focal point on your buffet table with a medley of fruits piled high on a crystal plate.

supplies

Table knife

12-inch-tall green plastic-foam
cone with 4-inch base

Toothpicks

Wood glue

Miniature artificial or fresh pears
and plums, kumquats,
blueberries, and cranberries

Grape leaves

Footed crystal cake plate
or compote

1. Use a table knife to trim off the tip of a plastic-foam cone. Put a generous amount of wood glue on the entire length of a toothpick. Insert one toothpick end into a pear and the opposite end into the cone top. Continue attaching the pears to the cone in rows, working from the top to the bottom.

2. Fill in the gaps between the pears with plums, then kumquats, attaching them in the same manner as the pears.

3. Finish the display with blueberries and cranberries, using toothpicks cut in half for attaching the fruit to the base.

4. Randomly tuck grape leaves into the arrangement, dabbing glue on the stems to secure them in place.

5. When the cone is covered with fruit as desired, let the glue dry. Place the cone onto a crystal cake plate or compote.

tabletop tree

Miniature tabletop Christmas trees make wonderful place-settings, hostess gifts, or dinner party favors.

1. For each tree, cut the florist's foam into a cube that almost fills the silver container. Place the foam into the container.

2. Trim the greenery sprigs to desired lengths. Push the end of each sprig into the foam center. Add water.

3. Cover the foam with Epsom salts for a snowy-looking base.

4. Thread beads onto wires and hang them on the tree to look like miniature ornaments.

supplies

Florist's foam

Scissors or knife

Small silver containers

Several 6- to 8-inch sprigs of
  greenery for each tree

Water

Epsom salts

Beads

Earring wires

bottlebrush trees

These petite trees, decked in snow flecks and sparkling trims, make an elegant grouping. To vary the forest height and depth, incorporate books and mirrors in the mix. Place larger trees into china bowls. Place smaller trees around the larger trees. If desired, wire miniature ornaments onto the trees.

earthly elegant topiary

Even if you're frazzled from the holiday hoopla, you'll have time to craft this simple topiary that takes its cue from Mother Nature.

supplies

Scissors; florist's foam

4-inch-tall, 6-inch-diameter
  silver bucket

Hot-glue gun and glue sticks

10-inch length of 1$^{3}/_{4}$-inch-
  diameter tree branch

12-inch-tall plastic-foam cone

Bun moss; thirty 1-inch-diameter
  silver ornaments; green sheet moss

2 yards of 1$^{1}/_{2}$-inch-wide silver
  wire-edge ribbon

1. Cut a block of florist's foam to fill the bucket. Hot-glue the foam to the inside bottom of the bucket.

2. Center one end of the tree branch in base of the plastic-foam cone. Insert the opposite end into the center of the florist's foam in the bucket. Adjust the branch depth until a trunk space of 4 inches remains between the bucket and the cone. Remove the branch and place glue on both ends; reinsert into the holes in the foam; let dry.

3. Cut the bun moss into small, round pieces. Hot-glue the moss pieces to the cone, covering it completely. Decorate the tree by gluing silver ornaments to the sides and top. Cover exposed florist's foam in bucket with green sheet moss; hot-glue in place. Tie silver ribbon into a bow and glue it to the sheet moss.

packed with punch,

A vintage punch bowl set, with its aged patina, provides an unexpected "convention center" for a gathering of jolly Santas. Place tinsel garland in the bottom of the bowl as a cushion, then arrange the tall fellows in back and the shorter elves up front.

initial wreath

Put your mark on the front door with a wreath in the shape of your family initial.

supplies

Computer (optional)

Paper; pencil; scissors

Sheets of plastic foam to make
  the desired size wreath

Hot-glue gun and glue sticks

U-shape floral pins; paring knife

Newspapers

Green spray paint for foam

Medium weight wire; wire cutters

Greenery

1. To make an initial pattern, use an enlarged computer font as a guide for the shape, or draw your own. Cut out the pattern.

2. If necessary, join several sheets of plastic foam by hot-gluing them together and using U-shape floral pins to further secure the seams. Place the pattern onto the foam. Trace around the shape and remove the pattern. Use a paring knife to cut the initial shape from foam.

3. In a well-ventilated work area, cover the work surface with newspapers. Spray-paint the foam cutout green. Let dry.

4. Wrap wire around the top of the initial for a hanger. Cut wire leaving long tails. Depending on the initial, you may want to cut a second piece of wire so the wreath hangs straight. Make a 1-inch loop in the center of each wire, twisting wire to secure. With the tails hanging down, place the wires around the top section(s) of the wreath and twist the ends together to secure.

5. Cut small pieces of various greenery. Using U-shape floral pins, attach the greenery to completely cover the initial shape. To conceal the pins, attach one sprig under the ends of the next sprig.

pinecone tabletop wreath

Stubbly pinecones and shiny jingle bells create a lively contrast. To make the wreath with ease, start with a
14- to 16-inch moss-covered wreath form and divide it into equal quadrants. Hot-glue three concentric rows of
jingle bells between quarters on the wreath. Glue pinecones to the remaining wreath surface.

sweet treats

holiday blossoms

To mix in a hint of holiday flavor, add ¼ teaspoon of mint, peppermint, or almond extract along with the vanilla.

Prep: 20 minutes Chill: 1 hour Bake: 8 minutes per batch
Oven: 350°F Makes: about 24 cookies

1. In a large mixing bowl beat butter and cream cheese with an electric mixer on medium to high speed for 30 seconds. Add powdered sugar, baking powder, and salt. Beat until combined, scraping sides of bowl occasionally. Beat in egg and vanilla. Beat in as much of the flour as you can with the mixer. Stir in any remaining flour. Cover and chill dough about 1 hour or until easy to handle.

2. Shape dough into 1¼-inch balls. Roll balls in colored sugar. Place 2 inches apart on ungreased cookie sheet. With scissors, snip each ball in half from the top, cutting three-quarters of the way through. Snip each half twice, making six wedges. Gently fold down wedges to make a flower shape. Sprinkle a little additional colored sugar in the center of each.

3. Bake in a 350° oven for 8 to 9 minutes or until edges are firm and bottoms are very lightly browned. Immediately place a mint chocolate ball in the center of each cookie. Transfer to a wire rack and let cool.

ingredients

½ cup butter, softened

1 3-ounce package cream cheese, softened

1½ cups powdered sugar

½ teaspoon baking powder

¼ teaspoon salt

1 egg

½ teaspoon vanilla

2¼ cups all-purpose flour

   Colored sugar

   Pastel candy-coated mint chocolate balls

candy cane cookies

Taking the shape of a beloved Christmas symbol, these cookies feature an equally beloved ingredient—chocolate.

ingredients

⅓ cup shortening

⅓ cup butter, softened

¾ cup sugar

1 teaspoon baking powder

1 egg

2 tablespoons milk

1 teaspoon vanilla

⅓ cup unsweetened cocoa powder

1¾ cups all-purpose flour

4 ounces white baking chocolate

2 to 4 teaspoons shortening

½ to ⅔ cup crushed peppermint candy canes

Prep: 30 minutes Chill: 1 hour Bake: 7 minutes per batch
Stand: 30 minutes Oven: 375°F Makes: about 36 cookies

1. In a medium mixing bowl beat the ⅓ cup shortening and the butter with an electric mixer on medium speed for 30 seconds. Add sugar and baking powder. Beat until combined, scraping sides of bowl occasionally. Beat in egg, milk, and vanilla. Beat in cocoa powder and as much of the flour as you can with the mixer. Stir in any remaining flour. Divide dough in half. Cover and chill about 1 hour or until easy to handle.

2. On a lightly floured surface roll one portion of dough to slightly less than ¼ inch thick. Using a 4-inch candy-cane-shaped cutter, cut out dough. Place cutouts 1 inch apart on an ungreased cookie sheet. Bake in a 375° oven for 7 to 9 minutes or until firm and light brown. Transfer to a wire rack and let cool. Repeat with remaining dough.

3. In a small saucepan heat white baking chocolate and 2 teaspoons shortening over low heat until melted, stirring often. (Add more shortening, if necessary, to make a mixture of drizzling consistency.) Drizzle a few cookies with baking chocolate mixture; sprinkle with crushed candy canes. Repeat with remaining cookies. Let cookies stand until set.

pastel cream wafers

High-sparkle coarse sugar is available by mail or where cake decorating supplies are sold. You can also sprinkle with more powdered sugar, if desired.

Prep: 30 minutes   Bake: 8 minutes per batch

Oven: 375°F   Makes: about 20 sandwiches

ingredients

½   cup cold butter

1   cup all-purpose flour

¼   cup half-and-half or
light cream

Coarse sugar or granulated
sugar

Powdered Sugar Frosting

1. In a medium mixing bowl cut butter into flour until pieces are the size of small peas. Sprinkle 1 tablespoon of the cream over part of mixture. Gently toss with a fork and push to side of bowl. Repeat until all of the flour mixture is moistened. Gently work mixture with hands and shape into a ball.

2. On a lightly floured surface roll dough to slightly less than ⅛ inch thick. With a scalloped 1¾-inch round cookie cutter, cut out dough. Place coarse sugar in a shallow dish. Press one side of each cutout into sugar to lightly coat. Place cutouts sugared sides up 1 inch apart on ungreased cookie sheet. With a fork, prick four parallel rows in each cutout.

3. Bake in a 375° oven for 8 to 10 minutes or until edges just begin to brown. Transfer to a wire rack and let cool.

4. Spread about 1 teaspoon Powdered Sugar Frosting on the flat side of half of the cookies. Top with the remaining cookies, flat sides down.

Powdered Sugar Frosting: In a small bowl combine 1 cup powdered sugar, 1 tablespoon softened butter, ½ teaspoon vanilla, 1 drop desired color food coloring, and enough half-and-half or light cream (3 to 4 teaspoons) to make a frosting of spreading consistency. Makes about ½ cup.

swedish butter cookies

Use real butter for the best results in these super-moist melt-in-your-mouth morsels.

ingredients

1½ cups all-purpose flour

2 tablespoons granulated sugar

1 teaspoon baking powder

1 cup butter

½ cup half-and-half or
   light cream

   Coarse sugar or granulated
   sugar

Prep: 20 minutes Chill: 1 hour Bake: 12 minutes per batch
Oven: 350°F Makes: about 40 cookies

1. In a large bowl combine flour, 2 tablespoons sugar, and baking powder. Using a pastry blender, cut in butter until mixture resembles coarse crumbs. Add half-and-half, stirring with a fork until dough clings together. Form dough into a ball. Cover and chill dough about 1 hour or until easy to handle.

2. On a lightly floured surface, roll dough into a 10×8-inch rectangle. Cut into 2×1-inch sticks. Place 1 inch apart on ungreased cookie sheets.

3. With a small sharp knife, make ½-inch-long slashes on one of the long sides of each cookie, spacing slashes about ½ inch apart. Curve cookies slightly. Sprinkle with the coarse sugar.

4. Bake in a 350° oven about 12 minutes or until lightly browned. Cool for 1 minute on cookie sheet. Transfer to a wire rack and let cool.

sesame pecan wafers

Serve these nutty, Southern-style wafers to complement a generous scoop of your favorite ice cream.

Prep: 30 minutes Chill: 1 hour Bake: 7 minutes per batch
Oven: 375°F Makes: about 80 cookies

1. In a large mixing bowl beat butter with an electric mixer on medium to high speed for 30 seconds. Add sugar and vanilla. Beat until combined, scraping sides of bowl occasionally. Beat in as much of the flour as you can with the mixer. Stir in any remaining flour, sesame seeds, and pecans. Divide dough in half. If dough is sticky, wrap each half in waxed paper or plastic wrap and chill about 1 hour or until dough is easy to handle.

2. On a lightly floured surface, roll half of the dough to ⅛ inch thick. Using 2-inch cookie cutters, cut out dough into desired shapes. Place cutouts 1 inch apart onto ungreased cookie sheets.

3. Bake in a 375° oven for 7 to 8 minutes or until edges are lightly browned. Transfer to a wire rack and let cool. Repeat with remaining dough.

4. In a heavy small saucepan combine semisweet chocolate and shortening. Heat over low heat until melted, stirring occasionally. Drizzle melted chocolate over cookies. Let cookies stand until chocolate is set.

ingredients

1 cup butter, softened

⅔ cup sugar

1 teaspoon vanilla

1¾ cups all-purpose flour

½ cup sesame seeds

½ cup ground pecans
    or almonds

2 ounces semisweet chocolate

½ teaspoon shortening

gingerbread people

ingredients

- 3 cups all-purpose flour
- ³/₄ teaspoon baking soda
- ¹/₂ teaspoon ground cinnamon
- ¹/₈ teaspoon ground cloves
- ¹/₂ cup butter
- ¹/₂ cup sugar
- 1 egg
- ¹/₂ cup molasses
- 1 teaspoon vanilla
- ¹/₄ cup grated fresh ginger
  Royal Icing

Reindeer Cookies: Prepare recipe as above. In step 2, use 3- to 3¹/₂-inch reindeer cookie cutters to cut out dough. Place half of the cookies with the reindeer facing right and the other half with the reindeer facing left. Bake as directed. Decorate with icing as desired. Let icing dry completely. To assemble, spread bottoms of half of the reindeer cookies with Royal Icing. Place remaining reindeer cookies, bottom sides down, decorated sides facing out. *Pictured on the cover.*

Prep: 30 minutes Chill: 3 hours Bake: 5 minutes per batch
Oven: 375°F Makes: about 25 cookies

1. In a medium bowl combine flour, baking soda, cinnamon, and cloves; set aside. In a large mixing bowl beat butter with an electric mixer on medium to high speed for 30 seconds. Add sugar; beat until fluffy. Beat in egg, molasses, and vanilla. Beat in ginger and as much of the flour mixture as you can with the mixer. Stir in any remaining flour mixture. Cover and chill dough about 3 hours or until easy to handle.

2. On a lightly floured surface roll dough to ¹/₈ inch thick. Using 5-inch gingerbread people cookie cutters, cut out dough. Place cutouts about 1 inch apart on lightly greased cookie sheets.

3. Bake in a 375° oven for 5 to 6 minutes or until edges are firm and bottoms are light brown. Transfer to a wire rack and let cool. Pipe designs on cookies with tinted Royal Icing.

Royal Icing: In a large mixing bowl combine one 16-ounce package powdered sugar (about 4¹/₂ cups) , 3 tablespoons meringue powder, and ¹/₂ teaspoon cream of tartar. Add ¹/₂ cup warm water and 1 teaspoon vanilla. Beat with an electric mixer on low speed until combined; beat on high speed for 7 to 10 minutes or until very stiff. To tint, divide the icing into small portions. Add enough food coloring to each portion to make desired colors.

mitten cookies

These delicious cookies don't have to be decorated with the shape of a mitten. Decorate with other favorite holiday motifs such as reindeer, trees, or wreaths.

ingredients

1½   cups butter, softened

1⅔   cups granulated sugar

2   teaspoons baking powder

½   teaspoon salt

2   eggs

¼   cup buttermilk

½   teaspoon vanilla

⅓   cup ground toasted almonds

4   cups all-purpose flour

     Coarse colored sugars

Prep: 30 minutes Chill: 2 hours Bake: 14 minutes per batch
Oven: 375°F Makes: 16 large cookies

1. In a large mixing bowl beat butter with an electric mixer on medium to high speed for 30 seconds. Add granulated sugar, baking powder, and salt. Beat until combined, scraping sides of bowl occasionally. Beat in eggs, buttermilk, and vanilla. Beat in ground almonds and as much of the flour as you can with the mixer. Stir in any remaining flour. Cover and chill about 2 hours or until dough is easy to handle.

2. Using ⅓ cup dough for each cookie, shape dough into balls. Place on ungreased cookie sheet; cover with plastic wrap and flatten with hand or bottom of a pie plate to 4- to 5-inch rounds, spacing 1½ inches apart. Place a mitten cookie cutter or a stencil* onto a cookie; sprinkle colored sugar inside the cutter or stencil. Remove and repeat with remaining cookies.

3. Bake in a 375° oven about 14 minutes or until edges are firm and bottoms are browned. Cool for 2 to 3 minutes on cookie sheet. Transfer to a wire rack and let cool.

Mitten Stencil: Trace a mitten shape about 3 inches long on heavy cardboard or on the back of a stiff paper plate. Cut out mitten with a sharp knife.

pecan snaps with espresso cream

Elegant and sumptuous these are special occasion cookies. Prepare the coffee-spiked cream and fill the cones just before serving. If desired, sprinkle with grated chocolate.

Prep: 35 minutes Bake: 7 minutes per batch
Oven: 350°F Makes: about 30 small or 11 large cookies

1. Lightly grease a cookie sheet or line it with foil; set aside. In a small bowl combine brown sugar, melted butter, corn syrup, and coffee liqueur. Stir in pecans and flour until combined. Drop batter by level teaspoons 3 inches apart, or level tablespoons 5 inches apart, onto prepared cookie sheet. (Bake only 4 or 5 cookies at a time.)

2. Bake in a 350° oven for 7 to 8 minutes for smaller cookies or 8 to 10 minutes for larger cookies or until cookies are bubbly and a deep golden brown.

3. Cool cookies on the cookie sheet for 1 to 2 minutes or until set. Quickly remove 1 cookie; roll cookie around a metal cone or the greased handle of a wooden spoon. When the cookie is firm, slide the cookie off the cone or spoon and cool completely on a wire rack. Repeat with remaining cookies, 1 at a time. (If cookies harden before you can shape them, reheat them in the oven about 1 minute or until softened.)

4. Up to 30 minutes before serving, in a large mixing bowl beat whipping cream, powdered sugar, and espresso powder with an electric mixer on low speed until stiff peaks form (tips stand straight). Pipe or spoon some of the espresso cream into each cookie. If desired, sprinkle with grated chocolate.

ingredients

¼ cup packed brown sugar

3 tablespoons butter, melted

2 tablespoons dark-colored
    corn syrup

1 tablespoon coffee liqueur

½ cup finely chopped pecans

¼ cup all-purpose flour

1 cup whipping cream

¼ cup powdered sugar

4 teaspoons instant
    espresso powder

Grated chocolate (optional)

fudgy fruitcake drops

The flavor of this cocoa-rich cookie—filled with nuts, raisins, and chocolate pieces—will "take the cake" in any holiday assortment of sweets.

Prep: 30 minutes Bake: 10 minutes per batch
Oven: 350°F Makes: about 48 cookies

1. In a medium bowl combine flour, cocoa powder, and baking powder; set aside. In a large mixing bowl beat butter with an electric mixer on medium speed for 30 seconds. Add granulated sugar. Beat until combined, scraping sides of bowl occasionally. Beat in egg, grape jelly, and vanilla. Beat in flour mixture. Stir in nuts, raisins, and chocolate pieces.

2. Drop dough by rounded teaspoons 2 inches apart onto lightly greased cookie sheet. Bake in a 350° oven about 10 minutes or just until set. Cool for 1 minute on cookie sheet. Transfer to a wire rack and let cool. If desired, sift powdered sugar over cookies.

ingredients

1   cup all-purpose flour

¼   cup unsweetened cocoa powder

2   teaspoons baking powder

¼   cup butter, softened

½   cup granulated sugar

1   egg

½   cup grape jelly

1   teaspoon vanilla

2   cups chopped walnuts

1½   cups raisins

1   cup semisweet chocolate pieces

Powdered sugar (optional)

giant snickerdoodle cookies

The name might make you giggle, but the flavor of these big sugar cookies will make you swoon. Don't crowd the cookie sheet—they need room to expand.

ingredients

4½ cups all-purpose flour

2 teaspoons baking powder

1 teaspoon baking soda

¾ teaspoon salt

1¼ cups shortening

2½ cups sugar

2 eggs

1½ teaspoons vanilla

½ teaspoon lemon extract or
    1 teaspoon finely shredded
    lemon peel

1 cup buttermilk

2 tablespoons ground cinnamon

Prep: 20 minutes Chill: 4 hours Bake: 12 minutes per batch
Oven: 375°F Makes: about 24 cookies

1. In a medium bowl combine flour, baking powder, baking soda, and salt. In a large mixing bowl beat shortening with an electric mixer on medium to high speed for 30 seconds. Add 2 cups of the sugar. Beat until combined, scraping sides of bowl occasionally. Beat in eggs, one at a time, beating well after each addition. Stir in vanilla and lemon extract.

2. Beat the flour mixture and buttermilk alternately into creamed mixture, scraping sides of bowl occasionally. Cover and chill dough for at least 4 hours or until easy to handle.

3. In a small bowl combine the remaining ½ cup sugar and the cinnamon. For each cookie, use a ¼-cup measure or ¼-cup ice-cream scoop* and shape dough into balls. Roll balls in the sugar-cinnamon mixture to coat. Place 3 inches apart on lightly greased cookie sheet. With the palm of your hand, gently press down balls to ½-inch thickness.

4. Bake one batch at a time in a 375° oven for 12 to 14 minutes or until bottoms are a light gold. Transfer to a wire rack and let cool.

*Note: If using an ice-cream scoop, lightly coat the scoop with nonstick cooking spray to help prevent dough from sticking.

brown sugar icebox cookies

Use either light or dark brown sugar. Dark brown sugar results in a slightly darker, softer cookie with a stronger molasses flavor.

Prep: 30 minutes Chill: 4 hours Bake: 10 minutes per batch
Oven: 375°F Makes: 60 cookies

1. In a large mixing bowl beat shortening and butter with an electric mixer on medium to high speed for 30 seconds. Add brown sugar, baking soda, and salt. Beat until combined, scraping sides of bowl occasionally. Beat in egg and vanilla. Beat in as much of the flour as you can with the mixer. Stir in any remaining flour and the ¾ cup ground hazelnuts.

2. Divide dough in half. On waxed paper, shape each half into a 10-inch-long log. Lift and smooth the waxed paper to help shape the logs. If desired, roll logs in the ⅔ cup chopped nuts. Wrap each log in plastic wrap. Chill in the refrigerator at least 4 hours or until firm enough to slice.

3. Cut logs into ¼-inch-thick slices. Place slices 1 inch apart onto an ungreased cookie sheet. Bake in a 375° oven about 10 minutes or until edges are firm. Transfer to a wire rack and let cool. If desired, drizzle melted chocolate over cookies.

ingredients

½ cup shortening

½ cup butter, softened

1¼ cups packed brown sugar

½ teaspoon baking soda

¼ teaspoon salt

1 egg

1 teaspoon vanilla

2½ cups all-purpose flour

¾ cup ground hazelnuts or pecans, toasted

⅔ cup finely chopped hazelnuts or pecans, toasted (optional)

Milk chocolate, melted (optional)

walnut-anise gems

Compact walnut-studded balls with a hint of licorice flavor are reminiscent of the cookie-platter classic known as Mexican Wedding Cakes, Pecan Sandies, or Snowballs.

ingredients

1   cup butter, softened

1/3   cup extra-fine or regular granulated sugar

1½   teaspoons anise seeds, crushed

1   tablespoon water

1   teaspoon vanilla

2¼   cups all-purpose flour

1   cup finely chopped walnuts, toasted

1   cup sifted powdered sugar

Prep: 45 minutes Bake: 20 minutes per batch

Oven: 325°F Makes: about 60 cookies

1. In a large mixing bowl beat butter with an electric mixer on medium to high speed for 30 seconds. Add granulated sugar and anise seeds. Beat until combined, scraping sides of bowl occasionally. Beat in water, vanilla, and as much of the flour as you can with the mixer. Stir in any remaining flour and the walnuts with a wooden spoon.

2. Shape dough into 1 inch balls. Place 1 inch apart on an ungreased cookie sheet.

3. Bake in 325° oven for about 20 minutes or until bottoms are lightly browned. Transfer to a wire rack and let cool. Gently shake cooled cookies in a plastic bag with the powdered sugar.

spritz

For colorful variations of these fun-shaped gems, tint portions of the dough with paste food coloring.

ingredients

½   cup butter, softened

1   cup granulated sugar

1   teaspoon baking powder

1   egg

1   teaspoon vanilla

¼   teaspoon almond extract
(optional)

3½   cups all-purpose flour

Colored sugar

Canned frosting (optional)

Confetti and/or candies
(optional)

Prep: 25 minutes Bake: 8 minutes per batch

Oven: 375°F Makes: about 84 cookies

1. In a large mixing bowl beat butter with an electric mixer on medium to high speed for 30 seconds. Add granulated sugar and baking powder. Beat until combined, scraping sides of bowl occasionally. Beat in egg, vanilla, and if desired, almond extract until combined. Beat in as much of the flour as you can with the mixer. Stir in any remaining flour.

2. Force unchilled dough through a cookie press onto an ungreased cookie sheet. If desired, sprinkle cookies with colored sugar. Bake in a 375° oven for 8 to 10 minutes or until edges are firm but not brown. Transfer to a wire rack and let cool. If desired, decorate unsugared cookies with frosting and confetti and/or candies.

Chocolate Spritz: Prepare as above, except reduce flour to 3¼ cups and add ¼ cup unsweetened cocoa powder with the sugar.

Nutty Spritz: Prepare as above, except reduce granulated sugar to ⅔ cup and flour to 3¼ cups. After adding flour, stir in 1 cup finely ground toasted almonds or hazelnuts (filberts).

peanut brittle cookies

Imagine the buttery flavor and delightful crunch of peanut brittle encased in a soft, chewy (and easy-to-make) oatmeal cookie.

Prep: 25 minutes Bake: 12 minutes per batch

Oven: 350°F Makes: about 24 cookies

1. Line two cookie sheets with foil and grease the foil; set aside.

2. In a large mixing bowl beat butter and shortening with an electric mixer on medium to high speed for 30 seconds. Add brown sugar, baking powder, and baking soda. Beat until combined, scraping sides of bowl occasionally. Beat in egg and vanilla. Beat in as much of the flour as you can with the mixer. Stir in any remaining flour. Stir in rolled oats, chopped chocolate, and ½ cup of the crushed peanut brittle.

3. Drop dough by rounded teaspoons 2 inches apart onto prepared cookie sheet. Flatten each mound slightly.

4. Bake in a 350° oven for 8 minutes. Remove cookie sheet from oven. Sprinkle each cookie with some of the remaining crushed peanut brittle, carefully pressing in slightly. Bake for 4 to 5 minutes more or until edges are lightly browned. Cool for 2 minutes on cookie sheet. Transfer to a wire rack and let cool.

ingredients

½ cup butter, softened

¼ cup shortening

1 cup packed dark brown sugar

½ teaspoon baking powder

¼ teaspoon baking soda

1 egg

1 teaspoon vanilla

1¼ cups all-purpose flour

1¼ cups quick-cooking rolled oats

4 ounces bittersweet or semisweet chocolate, chopped

1 cup crushed peanut brittle

yule logs

Symbolic of a Yule log on a blazing fire, these sweet and spicy little cookies add to the season's warmth and fellowship.

ingredients

1   cup butter, softened

¾   cup granulated sugar

¼   cup packed brown sugar

½   teaspoon ground ginger

¼   teaspoon ground nutmeg

1   egg

1   tablespoon dark rum

1   teaspoon vanilla

2¾ cups all-purpose flour

Browned-Butter Frosting

Ground nutmeg

Prep: 1 hour Chill: 30 minutes Bake: 12 minutes per batch
Oven: 350°F Makes: 40 cookies

1. In a large mixing bowl beat butter with an electric mixer on medium to high speed for 30 seconds. Add granulated sugar, brown sugar, ginger, and the ¼ teaspoon nutmeg. Beat until combined, scraping sides of bowl occasionally. Beat in egg, rum, and vanilla. Beat in as much of the flour as you can with the mixer. Stir in any remaining flour. Divide dough into eight portions. Wrap in plastic wrap; chill about 30 minutes or until dough is easy to handle.

2. On a lightly floured surface, shape each dough portion into a rope ½ inch thick (about 15 inches long). Cut ropes into 3-inch-long logs. Place logs 2 inches apart on ungreased cookie sheet.

3. Bake in a 350° oven about 12 minutes or until lightly browned. Transfer to a wire rack and let cool. Spread Browned-Butter Frosting over each cookie. Run a fork lengthwise along log so frosting resembles bark. Sprinkle lightly with ground nutmeg. Let frosting dry.

Browned-Butter Frosting: In a small saucepan heat ½ cup butter over low heat until melted. Continue heating until butter turns a delicate brown. Remove from heat; pour butter into a medium mixing bowl. Add 4½ cups powdered sugar, ¼ cup milk, and 2 teaspoons vanilla. Beat with an electric mixer on low speed until combined. Beat on medium to high speed, adding additional milk (1 to 2 tablespoons) as necessary.

eggnog thumbprints

Tender, walnut-encrusted, nutmeg-infused butter cookies serve as delicious vessels for a creamy, rum-flavored filling. Pipe in the filling just before serving so it holds its shape.

Prep: 45 minutes Chill: 1 hour Bake: 10 minutes per batch
Oven: 375°F Makes: about 40 cookies

1. In a large mixing bowl beat butter with an electric mixer on medium to high speed for 30 seconds. Add sugar and the ⅛ teaspoon nutmeg. Beat until combined, scraping sides of bowl occasionally. Beat in egg yolks and vanilla. Beat in as much of the flour as you can with the mixer. Stir in any remaining flour. Cover and chill for 1 hour or until dough is easy to handle.

2. Shape dough into 1-inch balls. Roll balls in egg whites, then in chopped walnuts to coat. Place balls 1 inch apart on lightly greased cookie sheet. Press your thumb into the center of each ball to make an indentation.

3. Bake in a 375° oven for 10 to 12 minutes or until edges are lightly browned. Transfer to a wire rack and let cool. Pipe or spoon about ½ teaspoon Rum Filling into the center of each cooled cookie. Sprinkle with nutmeg.

Rum Filling: In a small mixing bowl beat ¼ cup butter with an electric mixer on medium speed until softened. Add 1 cup powdered sugar and beat until fluffy. Beat in 1 teaspoon rum or ¼ teaspoon rum extract and enough milk (1 to 2 teaspoons) to make a filling of spreading consistency.

ingredients

¾   cup butter, softened

½   cup sugar

⅛   teaspoon ground nutmeg

2   egg yolks

1   teaspoon vanilla

1½ cups all-purpose flour

2   slightly beaten egg whites

1½ cups finely chopped walnuts

    Rum Filling

    Ground nutmeg

peanut butter bark

It is worth your while to search out raw peanuts for this bark; they are less likely to burn when stirred into the hot syrup.

Prep: 10 minutes Cook: 20 minutes

Makes: about 3 pounds or 48 servings

ingredients

2	cups peanut butter
1½	cups sugar
1½	cups light-colored corn syrup
¼	cup water
2	tablespoons butter
2	cups raw peanuts, toasted
1	teaspoon baking soda, sifted
1	teaspoon vanilla

1. In the top of a double boiler warm peanut butter over low heat. (Or warm peanut butter in a heatproof bowl set into a pan of warm water over low heat.) Meanwhile, butter two large baking sheets. Set aside.

2. Butter the sides of a 3-quart heavy saucepan. In saucepan combine sugar, corn syrup, and water. Cook and stir over medium-high heat until mixture boils. Clip a candy thermometer to side of pan. Cook and stir over medium-high heat until thermometer registers 270°F, soft-crack stage (about 15 minutes).

3. Reduce heat to medium. Add the butter, stirring until melted. Add peanuts. Cook and stir until candy starts to turn brown and thermometer registers 295°F, hard-crack stage (about 5 minutes). Remove pan from heat; remove thermometer.

4. Quickly sprinkle baking soda over mixture, stirring constantly. Stir in vanilla. Gently stir in warm peanut butter until combined.

5. Immediately pour onto prepared baking sheets. Working quickly, spread as thin as possible with a spatula. Cool completely; break into pieces. Store tightly covered for up to 1 week.

penuche

The name for this creamy, traditional candy comes from the Mexican word for "raw sugar" or "brown sugar."

Prep: 15 minutes Cook: 20 minutes Cool: 40 minutes

Makes: about 1¼ pounds (32 pieces)

1. Line an 8×4×2-inch loaf pan with foil, extending foil over edges of pan. Butter the foil; set pan aside.

2. Butter the sides of a 2-quart heavy saucepan. In saucepan combine granulated sugar, brown sugar, and half-and-half. Cook and stir over medium heat until mixture boils. Clip a candy thermometer to side of pan. Reduce heat to medium-low; continue boiling at a moderate, steady rate, stirring frequently, until thermometer registers 236°F, soft-ball stage (about 15 minutes). (Adjust heat as necessary to maintain a steady boil.)

3. Remove saucepan from heat. Add butter and vanilla, but do not stir. Cool, without stirring, to 110°F (about 40 minutes).

4. Remove thermometer from saucepan. Beat mixture vigorously with a clean wooden spoon until penuche just begins to thicken. Add the chopped pecans. Continue beating until penuche becomes thick and just starts to lose its gloss (about 10 minutes total).

5. Immediately spread penuche evenly into the prepared pan. Score into squares while warm. When penuche is firm, use foil to lift it out of pan. Cut penuche into squares. Store tightly covered for up to 1 week.

ingredients

- 1 cup granulated sugar
- 1 cup packed brown sugar
- ⅔ cup half-and-half or light cream
- 2 tablespoons butter
- 1 teaspoon vanilla
- ½ cup chopped pecans, walnuts, or cashews, toasted

white chocolate fudge

A batch of this light-colored fudge loaded with coconut and toasted almonds is a perfect gift for the sweet tooth on your list—of course, you'll love it too!

ingredients

2   cups white baking pieces
      (12 ounces)

1   cup sweetened condensed milk

8   ounces white baking
      chocolate, cut up

2   cups tiny marshmallows

1   teaspoon vanilla

½   cup flaked coconut

½   cup unblanched almonds,
      toasted and chopped

      Unblanched almonds, toasted
      and chopped (optional)

Prep: 25 minutes Chill: 2 hours

Makes: about 2 pounds or 6 dozen pieces

1. Line an 9×9×2-inch baking pan with foil, extending foil over edges of pan. Butter the foil; set pan aside.

2. In a 3-quart saucepan combine the white baking pieces, sweetened condensed milk, white baking chocolate, and marshmallows. Cook and stir over medium-low heat until completely melted.

3. Stir in vanilla, coconut, and the ½ cup almonds. Pour into prepared pan. Top with additional chopped almonds if desired.

4. Refrigerate for 2 hours or until firm. Lift from pan and remove foil. Cut into pieces.

Tip: For fudge to set up properly, at least one of the white chocolate products must contain cocoa butter.

latte fudge

Chocolate and espresso pair well in this decadent treat. This recipe makes about 5 dozen candies—plenty to share throughout the season.

Prep: 25 minutes Cook: 25 minutes Cool: 55 minutes

Makes: about 2 pounds (64 servings)

1. Line an 8×8×2-inch baking pan with foil, extending foil over edges of pan. Butter the foil; set pan aside.

2. Butter the sides of a 3-quart heavy saucepan. In saucepan combine sugar, half-and-half, espresso powder, corn syrup, and cinnamon. Cook and stir over medium-high heat until mixture boils. Clip a candy thermometer to side of pan. Reduce heat to medium-low; continue boiling at a moderate, steady rate, stirring occasionally, until thermometer registers 236°F, soft-ball stage (25 to 35 minutes). (Adjust heat as necessary to maintain a steady boil.)

3. Remove saucepan from heat. Add butter and vanilla, but do not stir. Cool, without stirring, to 110°F (50 to 60 minutes). Remove thermometer from saucepan. Beat mixture vigorously with a clean wooden spoon until it just begins to thicken; stir in nuts. Continue beating until fudge becomes very thick and stiff, and just starts to lose its gloss (about 10 minutes total).

4. Immediately spread fudge evenly into prepared pan. Score into squares while warm and if desired, press a coffee bean into each piece. When fudge is firm, use foil to lift it out of pan. Cut fudge into squares. Store tightly covered up to 1 week.

ingredients

3 cups sugar

1½ cups half-and-half
     or light cream

2 tablespoons instant espresso
    powder or 3 tablespoons
    instant coffee crystals

3 tablespoons light-colored
    corn syrup

¼ teaspoon ground cinnamon

2 tablespoons butter

1 teaspoon vanilla

1 cup chopped walnuts,
   toasted

   Coffee beans (optional)

triple chocolate truffles

Three kinds of chocolate contribute to these elegant, party-worthy truffles. Serve on your prettiest platter.

Prep: 1 hour Chill: 3½ hours Makes: about 30 truffles

1. In a heavy medium saucepan cook and stir semisweet chocolate over very low heat until melted and smooth. Remove from heat; stir in cream cheese until combined. Combine coffee crystals and water; add to chocolate mixture and stir until smooth. Cover and chill truffle mixture about 2 hours or until firm.

2. Line a baking sheet with waxed paper. Use 2 spoons to shape the truffle mixture into 1-inch balls; place on prepared baking sheet. Cover and chill for 1 to 2 hours or until firm.

3. In a heavy medium saucepan cook and stir milk chocolate and shortening over low heat until melted and smooth. Remove from heat; cool to room temperature.

4. Use a fork to dip truffles into chocolate mixture, allowing excess chocolate to drip back into saucepan. Return truffles to baking sheet; chill about 30 minutes or until firm.

5. In a small heavy saucepan cook and stir white baking bar over low heat until melted and smooth. Drizzle over truffle tops. (Use white baking bar to drizzle over milk or semisweet chocolate truffles. Use milk or semisweet chocolate to drizzle over white baking bar truffles.) Before serving, chill for a few minutes or until set.

ingredients

12 ounces semisweet chocolate, coarsely chopped

½ of an 8-ounce package cream cheese, softened and cut up

4 teaspoons instant coffee crystals

1 teaspoon water

1⅓ cups milk chocolate or semisweet chocolate pieces, or 8 ounces white baking bar, coarsely chopped

2 tablespoons shortening

2 ounces white baking bar, milk chocolate, or semisweet chocolate, coarsely chopped

champagne truffles

Look for edible luster dust in the baking aisle of large supermarkets, specialty food stores, or craft stores.

ingredients

6   ounces semisweet chocolate, coarsely chopped

¼   cup butter, cut into small pieces

3   tablespoons whipping cream

1   egg yolk

3   tablespoons champagne or whipping cream

    Unsweetened cocoa powder or powdered sugar

    Edible luster dust (optional)

Prep: 45 minutes Chill: 2½ hours Makes: about 25 truffles

1. In a medium heavy saucepan combine semisweet chocolate, butter, and whipping cream. Heat over medium-low heat until chocolate is melted, stirring constantly. Gradually stir about half of the chocolate mixture into the egg yolk. Return entire mixture to the saucepan. Cook and stir over medium heat for 2 minutes more. Remove from heat. Stir in champagne. Transfer truffle mixture to a small bowl. Cover and chill about 1 hour or until thickened, stirring once or twice.

2. Beat cooled truffle mixture with an electric mixer on medium speed for 1 minute (color will lighten and mixture will be slightly fluffy). Cover and chill about 30 minutes or until mixture holds a mounded shape, but is not completely firm. Line a baking sheet with waxed paper. Using a small ice cream scoop or two small spoons, scoop mixture onto prepared baking sheet into 1-inch mounds. Cover and chill about 1 hour or until firm.

3. Lightly roll mounds between palm of hands to shape into balls. Roll truffles in cocoa powder. If desired, lightly brush truffles with edible luster dust.

nut rocha

Crunchy brittle coated with silken chocolate is the ultimate holiday indulgence. Serve in a cup and saucer as shown or give as a gift that everyone loves.

Start to Finish: 40 minutes Cool: Several hours

Makes: about 40 servings

1. Line a 15×10×1-inch baking pan with foil, extending foil over edges of pan; set aside.

2. In a 3-quart saucepan melt butter. Stir in sugar, corn syrup, and water. Bring to boiling over medium-high heat, stirring until sugar is dissolved. (Avoid splashing sides of pan.) Carefully clip a candy thermometer to pan. Cook over medium heat, stirring frequently, until thermometer registers 270°F, soft-crack stage (about 15 minutes). (Mixture should boil at a moderate, steady rate over entire surface.) Remove from heat; remove thermometer.

3. Pour mixture into prepared pan; spread evenly. Cool about 5 minutes or until top is set. Sprinkle with chocolate pieces; let stand for 2 minutes. Spread chocolate over candy. Sprinkle with nuts, pressing lightly into chocolate. Cool for several hours or until set.

4. Use foil to lift candy out of pan; break into pieces. Store tightly covered.

ingredients

2   cups butter

2   cups sugar

2   tablespoons light-colored
     corn syrup

1/3   cup water

1   11½-ounce package
     (1¾ cups) milk
     chocolate pieces

1   cup finely chopped nuts,
     toasted (such as almonds,
     pecans, walnuts,
     and/or cashews)

espresso-hazelnut biscotti

Delectable mocha-hazelnut flavored twice-baked cookies are marvelous dunked in tea or coffee. If desired dip one end of each biscotti into melted white chocolate.

ingredients

½ cup butter, softened

1 cup granulated sugar

2½ teaspoons baking powder

3 eggs

⅓ cup unsweetened cocoa powder

1 tablespoon instant espresso powder or 2 tablespoons instant coffee crystals

2¾ cups all-purpose flour

½ cup miniature semisweet chocolate pieces

½ cup chopped hazelnuts, toasted

1 egg white

1 teaspoon water

1 tablespoon coarse or granulated sugar

Prep: 30 minutes Bake: 38 minutes Cool: 30 minutes
Oven: 350°F/325°F Makes: about 36 biscotti

1. In a large mixing bowl beat butter with an electric mixer on medium to high speed for 30 seconds. Add the 1 cup granulated sugar and the baking powder. Beat until combined, scraping sides of bowl occasionally. Beat in eggs. Beat in cocoa powder, espresso powder or coffee crystals (if using coffee crystals, first dissolve in 1 teaspoon water), and as much of the flour as you can with the mixer. Stir in any remaining flour, chocolate pieces, and nuts.

2. Divide dough in half. Shape each portion into an 11-inch-long loaf. Place loaves 5 inches apart onto a lightly greased cookie sheet. Flatten loaves until 2¼ to 2½ inches thick. Combine egg white and the water. Brush over loaves. Sprinkle with coarse sugar.

3. Bake in a 350° oven about 25 minutes or until firm and a wooden toothpick inserted near center comes out clean. Cool on cookie sheet for 30 minutes or until completely cool.

4. Transfer loaves to a cutting board and cut each loaf diagonally into ½-inch-thick slices. Place slices cut sides down onto an ungreased cookie sheet. Bake in a 325° oven for 8 minutes. Turn slices over and bake for 5 to 10 minutes more or until dry and crisp (do not overbake). Transfer to a wire rack and let cool.

holiday biscotti

Serve these rich slices of biscotti with flavored coffee to holiday guests, or wrap them up to give as gifts.

Prep: 30 minutes Bake: 55 minutes Chill: 1 hour
Cool: 1 hour Oven: 350°F/325°F Makes: about 28

1. In a large mixing bowl beat butter with an electric mixer on medium to high speed for 30 seconds. Add sugar, baking powder, baking soda, and salt. Beat until combined, scraping sides of bowl occasionally. Beat in 3 of the eggs, vanilla, and almond extract. Beat in as much of the flour as you can with the mixer. Stir in any remaining flour, anise and fennel seeds, cranberries, pistachios, and apricots with a wooden spoon. Cover and refrigerate for 1 hour or until dough is easy to handle (dough will be slightly sticky).

2. Divide dough in half. Wet hands lightly with water and shape each half into a 12-inch-long log 1½ inches in diameter. Place 4 inches apart on a lightly greased cookie sheet. Flatten each log slightly to ¾-inch thickness. Combine remaining 1 egg and the water. Brush over logs.

3. Bake in a 350° oven for 25 to 30 minutes or until light brown. Cool on cookie sheet for 1 hour or until completely cool.

4. Transfer logs to a cutting board and cut each log diagonally into ½-inch-thick slices. Place slices cut sides down onto an ungreased cookie sheet. Bake in a 325° oven for 15 minutes. Turn slices over and bake about 15 minutes more or until golden brown. Biscotti will feel soft to the touch, but will become dry and crisp as they cool. Transfer to a wire rack and let cool.

ingredients

¼ cup butter, softened

1 cup sugar

1 teaspoon baking powder

½ teaspoon baking soda

¼ teaspoon salt

4 eggs

½ teaspoon vanilla

¼ teaspoon almond extract

2¼ cups all-purpose flour

1½ teaspoons anise seed

½ teaspoon fennel seed

1 cup dried cranberries

¾ cup pistachio nuts

½ cup dried apricots, snipped

1 tablespoon water

patchwork mittens

Patchwork cookies warm hearts as surely as real mittens warm fingers.

ingredients

½   cup butter, softened

1   3-ounce package cream
      cheese, softened

1½   cups sifted powdered sugar

½   teaspoon baking powder

¼   teaspoon salt

1   egg

½   teaspoon vanilla

2¼   cups all-purpose flour

      Paste food coloring

      Clear edible glitter

Prep: 1 hour Bake: 8 minutes per batch Chill: 1 hour
Oven: 375°F Makes: about 18 cookies

1. In a large mixing bowl beat butter and cream cheese with an electric mixer on medium speed for 30 seconds. Add powdered sugar, baking powder, and salt. Beat until combined, scraping sides of bowl occasionally. Beat in egg and vanilla. Beat in as much of the flour as you can with the mixer. Stir in any remaining flour.

2. Divide dough into five equal portions; place each portion into an individual bowl. Add desired paste food coloring to four portions, stirring or kneading until dough is evenly colored. Wrap each portion in plastic wrap or waxed paper. Chill dough about 1 hour or until easy to handle.

3. On a lightly floured surface, roll one portion of the dough at a time until ⅛ inch thick. Cut into 1-inch-wide strips with a fluted pastry wheel; cut dough strips into squares, diamonds, and triangles. Overlap dough pieces in groups of about 10 on an ungreased cookie sheet. Each group of pieces should be slightly larger than a 3-inch mitten-shaped cookie cutter. With the floured mitten-shaped cutter, cut out dough. (Reserve scraps; reroll to make marble cutouts.)

4. Bake in a 375° oven for 8 to 9 minutes or until edges are firm and bottoms are very lightly browned. Immediately sprinkle with edible glitter. Transfer cookies to a wire rack and let cool.

maple oatmeal bread

This hearty bread is a chewy choice for the Christmas-morning bread basket or holiday ham dinner.

ingredients

1   package active dry yeast

1¼   cups warm water
     (120°F to 130°F)

⅓   cup maple syrup

1   tablespoon cooking oil

1   teaspoon salt

1   cup quick-cooking
     rolled oats

2¾ to 3¼ cups bread flour

     Quick-cooking rolled oats

Prep: 25 minutes Rise: 1½ hours Bake: 35 minutes
Oven: 350°F Makes: 2 loaves (24 servings)

1. In a large bowl sprinkle yeast over warm water; let stand 5 minutes. Stir in maple syrup, cooking oil, salt, and the 1 cup oats. Stir in 2½ cups of the bread flour, a little at a time, until dough begins to form a ball.

2. Turn out onto a lightly floured surface. Knead in enough of the remaining bread flour to make a moderately stiff dough that is smooth and elastic. Shape dough into a ball. Place into a lightly greased bowl, turning once to grease dough surface. Cover; let rise in a warm place until double in size (about 1 hour).

3. Punch down dough. Turn out onto a lightly floured surface. Divide in half. Cover; let rest 10 minutes. Meanwhile, grease two 8×4×2-inch loaf pans.

4. Shape dough by gently patting and pinching each portion into a loaf shape, tucking edges beneath. Place into prepared pans. Sprinkle with oats. Cover; let rise in a warm place until nearly double in size (30 to 45 minutes).

5. Bake in a 350° oven 35 to 40 minutes or until bread sounds hollow when lightly tapped. (If necessary, cover loosely with foil the last 10 minutes of baking to prevent overbrowning.) Immediately remove bread from pans. Cool on wire racks.

cherry-pecan bread

Fruity nut-studded loaves are perfect for a holiday tea along with your favorite cookies. Prepare in advance and freeze, then just thaw and glaze before serving.

Prep: 25 minutes Bake: 1 hour

Oven: 325°F Makes: 2 loaves (28 servings)

1. Lightly coat two 8×4×2-inch loaf pans with cooking spray; set aside. Drain the maraschino cherries, reserving 2 tablespoons of the juice. Chop the cherries (to yield about ¾ cup chopped cherries). In a medium bowl combine the chopped cherries, ¼ cup of the flour, the pecans, and coconut; set aside.

2. In a large mixing bowl beat cream cheese and butter with an electric mixer on medium speed until smooth. Gradually add granulated sugar, beating until light and fluffy. Add eggs, one at a time, beating well after each addition. In a small bowl combine the remaining 1¾ cups flour and the baking powder; gradually beat into cream cheese mixture. Beat in vanilla. Fold in cherry mixture. Spread batter into prepared pans.

3. Bake in a 325° oven about 1 hour or until a wooden toothpick inserted near centers comes out clean. Cool in pans on wire rack for 10 minutes. Remove from pans. Cool completely on wire rack. For easier slicing, wrap and store overnight.

4. In a small bowl, combine powdered sugar and enough of the reserved maraschino cherry juice to make a glaze of spreading consistency. Spread glaze over bread.

ingredients

  Nonstick cooking spray

  1 10-ounce jar
     maraschino cherries

  2 cups all-purpose flour

  ½ cup coarsely chopped pecans

  ½ cup flaked coconut

  1 8-ounce package cream
     cheese, softened

  ¾ cup butter, softened

  2 cups granulated sugar

  4 eggs

  1½ teaspoons baking powder

  1½ teaspoons vanilla

  1 cup sifted powdered sugar

dried cherry scones

Scones are biscuit-like quick breads that originated in Scotland. To produce tender, flaky results, be sure to use cold butter.

Prep: 25 minutes Bake: 10 minutes

Cool: 10 minutes Oven: 400°F Makes: 12 scones

1. In a small bowl pour enough boiling water over dried cherries to cover. Let stand for 5 minutes; drain well.

2. Meanwhile, in a large bowl combine flour, brown sugar, baking powder, salt, and baking soda. Using a pastry blender, cut in butter until mixture resembles coarse crumbs. Add drained cherries and orange peel; toss to coat. Make a well in the center of the flour mixture; set aside. In a small bowl combine egg yolk and sour cream. Add yolk mixture all at once to flour mixture. Using a fork, stir until combined (mixture may seem dry).

3. Turn dough out onto a lightly floured surface. Quickly knead dough by folding and gently pressing for 10 to 12 strokes or until dough is nearly smooth. Pat or lightly roll dough into a 7-inch circle. Cut into 12 wedges.

4. Place wedges 1 inch apart on an ungreased baking sheet. Bake in a 400° oven for 10 to 12 minutes or until light brown. Transfer to a wire rack and let cool for 10 minutes. Drizzle with Orange Glaze. Serve warm.

Orange Glaze: In small bowl combine 1 cup powdered sugar, 1 tablespoon orange juice, and ¼ teaspoon vanilla. Stir in enough additional orange juice, 1 teaspoon at a time, to make glaze of drizzling consistency.

ingredients

½ cup snipped dried cherries

2 cups all-purpose flour

3 tablespoons packed brown sugar

2 teaspoons baking powder

½ teaspoon salt

½ teaspoon baking soda

¼ cup butter, cut into pieces

1 teaspoon finely shredded orange peel

1 beaten egg yolk

1 8-ounce carton dairy sour cream

Orange Glaze

orange nut loaf

Bring out the best in this citrus-accented bread by serving it with honey butter or whipped cream cheese.

Prep: 25 minutes Bake: 50 minutes
Oven: 350°F Makes: 1 loaf (16 servings)

1. Grease the bottom and halfway up the sides of an 8×4×2-inch loaf pan; set aside. In a medium bowl combine flour, sugar, baking powder, and salt; set aside.

2. In a large bowl combine egg, milk, orange peel, orange juice, and melted butter. Add flour mixture to egg mixture. Stir just until moistened (batter should be lumpy). Fold in nuts. Spoon batter into prepared pan.

3. Bake in a 350° oven for 50 to 60 minutes or until a wooden toothpick inserted near the center comes out clean. Cool in pan on a wire rack for 10 minutes. Remove from pan. Cool completely on a wire rack. Wrap in plastic wrap and store overnight before slicing.

ingredients

3   cups all-purpose flour

3/4   cup sugar

4   teaspoons baking powder

1   teaspoon salt

1   beaten egg

1   cup milk

2   to 3 teaspoons finely
      shredded orange peel

1/4   cup orange juice

2   tablespoons butter, melted

3/4   cup chopped walnuts,
      toasted

cranberry-orange ring

From orange to cranberry and cinnamon to cloves, this glazed ring embraces the season's vibrant colors and flavors.

ingredients

Prep: 40 minutes Rise: 1¼ hours Bake: 20 minutes

Cool: 1 hour Oven: 350°F Makes: 1 ring (16 servings)

¾   cup snipped dried cranberries

2   tablespoons orange juice

1   16-ounce loaf frozen sweet roll dough, thawed

3   teaspoons butter, melted

1   teaspoon finely shredded orange peel

¼   cup packed brown sugar

2   tablespoons finely chopped pecans, toasted

1   tablespoon all-purpose flour

¼   teaspoon ground cinnamon

¼   teaspoon ground nutmeg

⅛   teaspoon ground cloves

Orange Glaze (see recipe, page 68)

1. Line a large baking sheet with foil; grease foil. Set aside. In a medium bowl combine cranberries and orange juice; set aside.

2. On a lightly floured surface roll dough into a 15×9-inch rectangle (if dough is difficult to roll, let it rest a few minutes and try again). Brush with the 2 teaspoons of the melted butter. Drain cranberries; return cranberries to bowl. Add orange peel, brown sugar, pecans, flour, cinnamon, nutmeg, and cloves to cranberries; mix well. Sprinkle cranberry mixture evenly over dough.

3. Starting from a long side, roll up into a spiral; seal edge. Place seam side down onto prepared baking sheet. Bring ends together to form a ring. Moisten ends; pinch together to seal ring. Using kitchen scissors or a sharp knife, cut from the outside edge toward center, leaving about 1 inch attached. Repeat around the edge at 1-inch intervals. Gently turn each slice slightly so the same side of all slices faces upward.

4. Cover; let rise in a warm place until nearly double (1¼ to 1½ hours). Brush ring with the remaining 1 teaspoon melted butter.

5. Bake in a 350° oven about 20 minutes or until golden. Transfer ring to a wire rack and let cool 1 hour. Drizzle Orange Glaze over cooled ring.

chocolate pot de crème

Pretty little "pots" of pudding-like treats are sweet finales to a filling holiday meal.

Prep: 10 minutes Cook: 10 minutes

Chill: 4 hours Makes: 8 servings

1. In a medium heavy saucepan combine whipping cream, chocolate, and sugar. Cook and stir over medium heat about 10 minutes or until mixture comes to a full boil and thickens. (If chocolate flecks remain, use a rotary beater or wire whisk to beat mixture until blended.)

2. Gradually stir all of the hot mixture into the beaten egg yolks; stir in vanilla. Divide chocolate mixture evenly into 8 sake cups, small cups, pot de crème cups, or 3-ounce ramekins. Cover and chill for 4 to 24 hours before serving. If desired, garnish with white chocolate curls.

ingredients

- 2 cups whipping cream
- 6 ounces semisweet chocolate, coarsely chopped
- $\frac{1}{3}$ cup sugar
- 4 beaten egg yolks
- 1 teaspoon vanilla

  White chocolate curls (optional)

chocolate-cherry bread pudding

Make this luscious bread pudding irresistible with a dollop of whipping cream or vanilla ice cream.

Prep: 25 minutes Stand: 1 hour Bake: 1 hour
Cool: 1 hour Oven: 350°F Makes: 12 servings

1. In a small saucepan heat kirsch over medium-low heat just until simmering; remove from heat. Add cherries and let stand, covered, for 1 hour. Do not drain.

2. In a very large bowl toss bread with melted butter until coated. Divide half of bread cubes evenly between two 1½-quart baking dishes or place into one 3-quart rectangular baking dish. Sprinkle half of the chocolate evenly over bread in baking dishes; reserve remaining half of chocolate. Spoon half of the fruit and liquid evenly over the chocolate layer; reserve remaining half of fruit and liquid. Top with remaining bread.

3. In a large mixing bowl whisk together the eggs, milk, half-and-half, sugar, and vanilla until combined. Slowly pour egg mixture evenly over the layers in the baking dishes. Press down layers lightly.

4. Bake, covered, in a 350° oven for 45 minutes. Uncover and bake for 15 to 20 minutes more for the 1½-quart baking dishes (30 minutes more for the 3-quart baking dish) or until egg portion in center appears set. Sprinkle remaining chocolate and fruit with liquid evenly over the top. Let stand about 1 hour. Serve warm.

ingredients

⅔ cup kirsch or orange juice

1½ cups dried tart cherries, snipped

1 16-ounce loaf country Italian bread, cut into 1- to 1½-inch pieces (about 11 cups)

¼ cup butter, melted

8 ounces bittersweet chocolate, coarsely chopped

6 eggs, slightly beaten

3 cups milk

2 cups half-and-half

1 cup sugar

1 teaspoon vanilla

caramel apple crepes

If you want the flecks and flavor from vanilla beans, but want to avoid the preparation, use vanilla bean paste. Look for it in specialty food shops.

Prep: 15 minutes Cook: 20 minutes Makes: 4 servings

1. For crepes, in a blender container combine flour, water, milk, eggs, granulated sugar, and oil. Cover and blend until smooth, stopping and scraping the side of container as necessary.

2. Heat a lightly greased 6-inch skillet over medium heat; remove from heat. Spoon 2 tablespoons of the batter into skillet; lift and tilt skillet to spread batter evenly. Return skillet to heat; brown on one side only. Invert skillet over paper towels; remove crepe from skillet. Repeat with remaining batter.

3. Fold 12 crepes in half, browned side out. Fold in half again, forming a triangle. Place 3 crepes on each of 4 dessert plates. (To freeze remaining crepes, layer cooled crepes between sheets of waxed paper in an airtight container; freeze for up to 4 months. Thaw at room temperature for 1 hour before using.)

4. For sauce, in a large saucepan combine brown sugar and cornstarch. Stir in whipping cream, brandy, and butter. Add apples. Cook and stir over medium heat until thickened and bubbly. Cook and stir for 2 minutes more.

5. If desired, in a small bowl combine crème fraîche and vanilla bean paste. To serve, spoon warm apple sauce over crepes. Sprinkle with pecans. If desired, top with crème fraîche mixture.

ingredients

- $3/4$ cup all-purpose flour
- $1/3$ cup water
- $1/3$ cup milk
- 2 eggs
- 2 tablespoons granulated sugar
- 4 teaspoons walnut oil or cooking oil
- 1 cup packed brown sugar
- 4 teaspoons cornstarch
- 1 cup whipping cream
- 2 tablespoons apple brandy or brandy
- 1 tablespoon butter
- 2 cups thinly sliced, peeled apples (such as Granny Smith, Rome Beauty, or Jonagold)
- $1/2$ cup crème fraîche (optional)
- 1 teaspoon vanilla bean paste or vanilla (optional)
- $1/2$ cup toasted pecans, chopped

orange-champagne cakes

Angelette pans are simply small versions of angel food cake pans. Look for them in specialty cookware shops or substitute muffin cups.

Prep: 30 minutes Bake: 30 minutes Stand: 10 minutes
Oven: 325°F Makes: 12 cakes (each 3¼-inch)

1. Grease and flour two angelette pans or twelve 4-inch muffin cups; set aside. In a medium bowl combine cornmeal, flour, baking powder, and salt; set aside.

2. In a large mixing bowl beat butter with an electric mixer on medium to high speed for 30 seconds. Add 2 cups of the sugar; beat until combined. Add eggs, beat until combined. Beat in orange juice (mixture may appear curdled). Beat in cornmeal mixture just until combined. Fold in ground almonds and orange peel.

3. Spoon batter into prepared pans (about ⅔ cup batter for each muffin cup). Bake in a 325° oven about 30 minutes or until a wooden toothpick inserted near the centers comes out clean. Transfer to a wire rack and let cool in pans for 10 minutes.

4. Meanwhile, in a saucepan combine champagne and the remaining ¼ cup sugar. Bring to boiling, stirring to dissolve sugar. Reduce heat; simmer, uncovered, about 10 minutes or until mixture is reduced to 1 cup. Remove cakes from pans. Transfer warm cakes to a large platter, placing cakes bottoms-up. Prick cakes with a wooden toothpick. Carefully spoon or brush champagne syrup over cakes. Immediately cover cakes with plastic wrap; cool completely. Serve cakes at room temperature.

ingredients

1½   cups yellow cornmeal

1   cup all-purpose flour

2   teaspoons baking powder

⅛   teaspoon salt

1½   cups unsalted butter, softened

2¼   cups sugar

6   eggs, beaten

1   cup orange juice

3   cups finely ground almonds

1   tablespoon finely shredded
     orange peel

1½   cups champagne

pumpkin tiramisu

This rendition of a classic Italian dessert is a grand finale for a holiday dinner. Serve with strong, hot coffee or tea.

Prep: 40 minutes Chill: 6 hours Makes: 9 servings

1. In a small bowl combine the $2/3$ cup hot coffee and the brown sugar, stirring to dissolve sugar. Set aside. In a small saucepan combine the $1/2$ cup cooled coffee and the gelatin. Let stand for 5 minutes. Cook and stir over medium heat until gelatin is dissolved. Set aside.

2. In a large mixing bowl combine pumpkin, mascarpone cheese, the granulated sugar, the 2 teaspoons cinnamon, and the nutmeg; beat with an electric mixer on medium speed until smooth. While continuing to beat, gradually drizzle in gelatin mixture. Thoroughly wash and dry the beaters. In a chilled medium mixing bowl, beat 1 cup of the whipping cream with electric mixer on medium speed until soft peaks form (tips curl); fold into pumpkin mixture.

3. Arrange one-third of the ladyfinger halves in the bottom of a 2-quart square dish. Drizzle with one-third of the brown sugar mixture. Spoon one-third of the pumpkin mixture over ladyfingers. Repeat layers twice. Cover and chill for at least 6 hours or up to 24 hours.

4. To serve, in a chilled small mixing bowl beat the remaining $1/2$ cup whipping cream with chilled beaters of an electric mixer on medium speed until soft peaks form (tips curl). Spread over pumpkin layer. Sprinkle with ground cinnamon.

ingredients

$2/3$ cup hot brewed coffee

2 tablespoons packed
     brown sugar

$1/2$ cup brewed coffee, cooled

1 envelope unflavored gelatin

1 15-ounce can pumpkin

1 8-ounce carton
     mascarpone cheese

$1/2$ cup granulated sugar

2 teaspoons ground cinnamon

$1/4$ teaspoon ground nutmeg

$1\frac{1}{2}$ cups whipping cream

2 3-ounce package ladyfingers,
     split (24 total)

Ground cinnamon

very ginger pound cake

Sugar-sweetened kumquats and blood oranges lend their gorgeous color to the cake topping. Other citrus fruits can substitute as well.

ingredients

3 cups all-purpose flour

1 teaspoon baking powder

¼ teaspoon baking soda

¼ teaspoon salt

1 cup butter, room temperature

3½ cups granulated sugar

¾ cup packed brown sugar

2 tablespoons grated fresh ginger

2 teaspoons vanilla

5 eggs, room temperature

1 cup milk, room temperature

½ cup finely chopped candied or crystallized ginger (2.7-oz. jar)

1 cup water

3 blood oranges or oranges

12 kumquats

Prep: 70 minutes Bake: 60 minutes Oven: 350°F Makes: 16 servings

1. Grease and lightly flour a 10-inch tube pan. In a bowl stir together the flour, baking powder, baking soda, and salt; set aside. In a large mixing bowl beat the butter with a mixer on medium speed for 30 seconds. Gradually add 2 cups of the granulated sugar and the brown sugar, beating until well combined. Beat in fresh ginger and vanilla. Add eggs, one at a time, beating after each addition and scraping bowl frequently.

2. Add flour mixture and milk alternately to beaten mixture, beating on low speed after each addition just until combined. Gently stir in candied ginger. Pour batter into prepared pan. Bake in a 350° oven for 60 to 70 minutes or until a cake tester or wooden toothpick inserted near the center comes out clean. Cool in pan on a wire rack for 10 minutes. Remove cake from pan. Cool completely on rack.

3. For fruit topping, in a saucepan combine the water and the remaining 1½ cups granulated sugar. Bring to boiling. Boil gently for 15 to 20 minutes or until mixture forms a thick syrup, stirring occasionally. Stir more often as syrup begins to thicken. Meanwhile, thinly slice fruit and discard ends and any seeds. Add fruit to syrup, stirring to coat. Return to boiling. Reduce heat. Simmer, uncovered, about 5 minutes more or until fruit is just tender, gently turning fruit in syrup several times. Gently remove fruit from syrup with a slotted spoon. Continue to boil syrup, uncovered, for 10 to 15 minutes more or until reduced to ¾ cup. Cool about 15 minutes. Serve on a cake stand or serving plate. Spoon fruit topping over cake. Drizzle with syrup.

gingerbread-pear dessert

Here is a twist on everyone's favorite cheesecake–with a surprise gingerbread crust, pears, and a tangy touch of raspberry.

Prep: 45 minutes Bake: 1 hour Cool: 1 hour + 30 minutes

Chill: 2 hours Oven: 375°F/325°F Makes: 10 servings

1. In a large saucepan bring water, the ½ cup sugar, and the lemon juice to boiling. Add pears. Simmer, uncovered, for 5 minutes. Remove from heat. Stir in raspberry jam. Cool for 1 hour. (If desired, cover and chill up to 6 hours.) Drain.

2. Place gingerbread mix in a large bowl. Using a pastry blender, cut butter into mix until pieces are pea-sized. Stir in egg yolk just until combined. Remove and discard ½ cup gingerbread mixture. Press remaining mixture onto bottom of an ungreased 10-inch springform pan. Bake in a 375° oven for 25 minutes. Cool completely.

3. In a medium mixing bowl beat cream cheese with an electric mixer on medium to high speed for 30 seconds. Add the ⅓ cup sugar; beat until fluffy. Beat in eggs and vanilla. Spoon about half of the cheese mixture over crust. Spoon drained pears evenly over cheese mixture. Spoon remaining cheese mixture over pears.

4. Reduce oven temperature to 325°. Bake for 35 to 40 minutes or until center is set. Cool in pan for 30 minutes on a wire rack. Loosen sides of pan. Cover and chill for 2 to 24 hours. Remove sides of springform pan.

ingredients

- 2 cups water
- ½ cup sugar
- 2 tablespoons lemon juice
- 5 medium pears, peeled, cored, and sliced
- ⅓ cup seedless red raspberry jam
- 1 14½-ounce package gingerbread mix
- ½ cup butter, cut into pieces
- 1 egg yolk
- 1 8-ounce package cream cheese, softened
- ⅓ cup sugar
- 3 eggs
- ½ teaspoon vanilla

holiday pumpkin cheesecake

Pumpkin is the delicious star in this special dessert, as you'll discover in this decadent holiday cheesecake.

Prep: 35 minutes Bake: 1 hour + 8 minutes Cool: 1 ¾ hours

Chill: 4 hours Oven: 325°F Makes: 10 servings

1. For crust, in a medium bowl combine crumbs, ⅓ cup of the sugar, and melted butter. Press crumb mixture onto the bottom and about 2 inches up the sides of an ungreased 9-inch springform pan. Bake in a 325° oven for 8 minutes. Transfer to a wire rack and let cool.

2. For filling, in a large mixing bowl beat cream cheese, the remaining 1 cup sugar, the pumpkin, whipping cream, vanilla, and allspice beating on medium speed of an electric mixer until combined. Add eggs and beat on low speed until just combined. Spoon mixture into crust-lined pan.

3. Set springform pan into a shallow baking pan. Bake in a 325° oven about 1 hour or until center appears nearly set when gently shaken. Transfer to a wire rack and let cool in pan for 15 minutes. Loosen crust from sides of pan with a thin-bladed knife or narrow spatula and cool for 30 minutes more. Remove sides of pan; cool for 1 hour. Cover and chill at least 4 hours or up to 24 hours.

4. Just before serving, spoon caramel ice cream topping over top of cheesecake. If desired, garnish with currants and/or fresh berries.

ingredients

1½ cups graham cracker crumbs (about 20 squares)

1⅓ cups sugar

½ cup butter, melted

3 8-ounce packages cream cheese, softened

1 cup canned pumpkin

1 tablespoon whipping cream

1½ teaspoons vanilla

¾ teaspoon ground allspice

3 eggs, slightly beaten

½ cup caramel ice cream topping

Fresh currants and/or small berries (optional)

royal christmas cake

ingredients

- 2 cups all-purpose flour
- 1 teaspoon ground cinnamon
- $\frac{1}{2}$ teaspoon baking powder
- $\frac{1}{4}$ teaspoon baking soda
- $\frac{1}{4}$ teaspoon ground nutmeg
- $\frac{1}{4}$ teaspoon ground cloves
- $1\frac{1}{2}$ cups dried currants
- $1\frac{1}{2}$ cups dark or golden raisins
- $1\frac{1}{2}$ cups diced mixed candied fruits and peels
- 1 cup candied red and/or green cherries
- $\frac{1}{2}$ cup almonds, ground
- 4 eggs
- 1 cup sugar
- $\frac{3}{4}$ cup butter, melted
- $\frac{1}{2}$ cup rum or orange juice
- 3 tablespoons lemon juice
- Rum, brandy, or orange juice
- 1 8-ounce can almond paste
- Royal Icing (see recipe, page 40)

Prep: 45 minutes Bake: 1 hour Cool: 2 hours

Chill: 1 week Oven: 300°F Makes: 16 servings

1. Grease bottom and sides of two $9\times1\frac{1}{2}$-inch round baking pans. Line bottoms with waxed paper. Grease paper; sprinkle bottom and sides with flour; set aside. In a large bowl combine flour, cinnamon, baking powder, baking soda, nutmeg, and cloves. Stir in currants, raisins, fruits and peels, cherries, and almonds. Set aside.

2. In a medium bowl beat eggs with a fork. Add sugar, butter, $\frac{1}{2}$ cup rum, and lemon juice; stir until combined. Stir egg mixture into fruit mixture; pour into prepared pans. Bake in a 300° oven for 1 to $1\frac{1}{4}$ hours. Cool in pans on wire racks 20 minutes; loosen edges. Remove from pans. Cool thoroughly on wire racks. Wrap layers separately in cotton cheesecloth moistened with rum. Wrap with foil. Refrigerate 1 to 2 weeks. Remoisten cheesecloth with additional rum if it becomes dry, making sure it stands for at least a day after remoistening.

3. To assemble, up to 2 hours before serving, unwrap cakes. Place one cake layer, top side down, on a serving plate. Spread with half of the almond paste. (If paste is too thick to spread, divide in half and shape into balls. Place each ball between two sheets of waxed paper; flatten slightly. With a rolling pin, roll each portion into a $9\frac{1}{2}$-inch circle; trim to form a 9-inch circle. Remove paper from one circle; invert onto cake). Spread $\frac{3}{4}$ cup Royal Icing over almond paste on first cake layer. Add second cake layer, top side up; spread or top with remaining almond paste. Frost top and sides of cake with remaining Royal Icing. Let stand at least 30 minutes to allow icing to set. Serve within 2 hours of frosting.

wrap it up

merry motifs

Take your package topper cue from the design of the wrapping paper.

1. Wrap the boxed gift with wrapping paper.

2. Cut a length of ribbon to wrap around the box once allowing ends to overlap slightly. Arrange the ribbon on the wrapped gift and tape the ribbon ends on the bottom of the package.

3. Hot-glue the package topper where desired on the ribbon.

Another Tip or Two

• If fresh flower or greenery package toppers are desired, use a florist's vial to keep them healthy. Tuck a piece of water-moistened tissue paper into the vial before adding the flower or greenery.

• For more merry wrapping combinations, use snowman paper with a snowflake ornament topper, geometric paper with a plastic star topper, or Santa Claus paper with a topper made of miniature wrapped packages.

supplies

Boxed gift

Wrapping paper

Scissors

Tape

Narrow ribbon to coordinate with
   wrapping paper

Package topper in design taken
   from wrapping paper

Hot-glue gun and glue sticks

stunning in silver

Stir a little fun into your holiday by packaging gifts in shiny new paint cans gussied up with silvery sensations.

1. If desired, cushion the bottom of the paint can with a layer of paper shred. Place the tissue-wrapped gift into the paint can and secure the lid on the can.

2. Embellish the can with wide-ribbon bows, ornaments, jingle bells, or holiday picks, wiring in place if needed.

3. Use narrow ribbon or cord to tie the paint can opener on the handle of the paint can. Sturdy cans work especially well for protecting fragile gifts that have to be shipped.

supplies

Paper shred (optional)

Small tissue-wrapped gift

New silver paint cans
  (available in paint stores)

Wide silver ribbon

Silver plastic ornaments on wires

Silver jingle bells

Silver holiday picks; fine silver wire

Narrow silver ribbon or cord

Paint can opener

Another Tip or Two

• Use these shiny containers to deliver gifts of holiday snack mixes.

• For a child's gift, trim the container with bright small toys, hair bows, or wood beads and blocks.

for deer ones

A simple celluloid reindeer hanging from looped ribbon dresses up a green glass jar. Both the jar and ornament can be found at flea markets and antiques malls for the cost of a box, paper, and bow. Fill the jar with edible goodies or tuck in a bit of tissue paper and slip a small gift inside.

button tree

Ivory-color vintage buttons on natural or brown wrapping paper make a stylish yet romantic combination.

supplies

Vintage buttons or other buttons collected from flea markets and garage sales

Boxed gift wrapped in natural or brown wrapping paper

Hot-glue gun and glue sticks

Natural raffia

1. Hot-glue buttons to the top of a package in a tree shape.

2. Wrap several strands of raffia around package and tie the ends into a bow.

Note: To remove the buttons from the paper after unwrapping the gift, place the discarded gift wrap in a plastic freezer bag in the freezer; the buttons will pop off.

Another Tip or Two

• Draw a simple Santa face and use buttons to form his beard, mustache, and hat trim.

• Arrange green buttons in a circular shape for a wreath. Glue on a few small red buttons to resemble berries.

kissed by nature

Give packages old-fashioned simplicity with solid-color paper and natural trims. Look for papers at specialty paper stores. Tie with ribbon or twine, and tuck in fresh bay leaves, pepperberries, or cinnamon sticks. Drill holes in dried pomegranates and glue them to the twine ends.

razzle-dazzle rickrack

Purchased white boxes become dazzling gift containers when you add simple designs in gold rickrack. Use these boxes for inspiration to make your own using other decorative trim. Use small dabs of crafts glue to secure the trim.

scalloped gift tags

Snippets of paper trimmed with paper-punched lace edges make keepsake gift tags.

1. Using straight or decorative-edged scissors, cut a desired shape from the ivory or white paper. This piece of paper will bear the "To-From" writing or other written holiday message.

2. Using the gift tags, right, for inspiration, cut additional shapes from colored papers. To hold paper layers together, punch two holes through layers and weave a paper strip through the holes to secure.

3. To make a lacy edge, first cut the paper edge with a scalloped-edged scissors. Then, use a small paper punch to create holes within the scallops.

4. To decorate the tags, glue the decorative-shaped paper punches and tiny pieces that have been punched away into the cut shapes.

supplies

Scraps of paper in holiday colors and ivory or white

Straight and decorative-edged scissors (available in crafts and fabric stores)

Small round paper punch

Paper punches with desired shapes (available in crafts and discount stores)

Thick white crafts glue

glistening greetings

Silver and white stickers combine to make merry holiday greeting cards. Choose different sizes and fonts for interest. Press the large-size words onto plain card stock first and fill in the spaces with small letters.

window wonderland

Take a peek at what's showing through the windows of these cards made with pretty papers and punches.

1. Cut the decorative card stock to measure 8½×5½ inches. Punch a square opening in the front of each card ⅞ inch from the top and centered from side to side.

2. Punch a snowman, star, or snowflake from the shimmery card stock. Referring to the photograph, use a needle to pierce tiny hanging holes in the punched shapes. For the snowman, use the bottom button as one hole and make the second hole in the hat. For the star and snowflake, punch two holes opposite each other at top and bottom or side to side.

3. Center and tape the punches in the windows. Pierce holes close to the window edges so they align with the holes in the punches.

4. Thread the needle with an 8-inch length of thread. Working from the back of the card, sew through the window hole to the front of the card and back through the front of the punch. Tie the thread in a square knot. Repeat for the other holes. Slide the knots so they are positioned behind the card. Place a dot of glue on each knot, trim the thread ends, and remove the tape.

supplies

Decorative card stock; paper cutter or scissors and straightedge

Paper punches in ¹¹⁄₁₆-inch square, snowman silhouette, jumbo snowflake, and jumbo star

Shimmery card stock in white, silver, and gold

Needle; metallic threads in silver and gold

Clear low-tack tape for paper and framing, such as Scotch 811 tape

Quick-drying industrial-strength glue

tie-it-up gift cards

Large or small, any size card is festive when trimmed with a gift. Fill mini packages with potpourri to double as sachets.

supplies

Art paper

Scissors

Small piece of felt

Needle

Thread

Polyester stuffing or potpourri

Awl

Silver cording

1. Fold art paper to desired card size (the cards, left, are 5×5 and 4×9 inches), using a second color slightly smaller if desired.

2. Cut two pieces of felt, approximately 2½×2½ inches for a square package or 1¾×3½ inches for a rectangular package.

3. Using a running stitch and with wrong sides together, sew three sides of the felt together. Stuff with a small amount of batting. Sew the remaining side closed.

4. With an awl, poke small holes in the card front at the sides and the top and bottom of the gift. Lace silver cording through the holes, over gift, and tie in a bow. The potpourri-filled gifts double as sachets.

festive package trims

Make the gift wrap as special as the gift by topping packages with these creative bows and tags that are made quick as a wink.

1. Push dowel pieces into floral oasis about 5 inches apart. Holding the ribbon end on top of the oasis, wrap ribbon around dowels at least three times. For larger bows, wrap four to six times.

2. Cut the ribbon, leaving about an 8-inch tail. Slip ribbon tail underneath loops, continuing to hold the ribbon's starting end.

3. Secure the loops by tying the ribbon ends firmly into a knot in the center of the loops. Carefully slide the bow loops off the dowels.

4. Tie the bow atop intersecting ribbons that wrap around the package. Separate and fluff the loops. Fold the ribbon ends in half and trim on the diagonal.

supplies

Two 4-inch pieces of ¼-inch dowel

Floral oasis

Ribbon

Scissors

stocking surprise holders

Purchased holiday-trimmed socks are gifts and wrapping all in one. Just tuck special surprises inside and hide among the evergreen branches for little ones to discover on Christmas morning.

snow fella place setting

Set up the crafting table assembly-line fashion this year, making gifts for many friends all at one time.

1. Wash and dry the place mats and napkins. Do not use fabric softener, dryer sheets, or detergents with additives. Iron all the pieces.

2. Apply white paint near a corner of one place mat, creating three ball shapes for the snowman body. Extend small drifts of snow beyond the body. See the photograph, right, for details. Use a small brush to swirl and shape the paint, giving it a three-dimensional look. While the paint is still wet, sprinkle glitter over the surface. Let the paint dry completely, then shake off the excess glitter. Repeat for the other place mats. For interest, make some snowmen in pairs and alternate sides and figure placement. Paint a snowman in one corner of each napkin.

3. Glue seed beads to the face for eyes. Cut a tiny triangle of orange felt for the nose and glue it in place. Add ribbons for scarves. If desired, use more seed beads for buttons.

4. Using black paint, draw black hats on the snowmen, altering the shapes to fit their personalities. Embellish the hats with dots of red and green paint, painted sprigs of holly, or other trims.

5. Add twig arms and hands using long stitches of perle cotton. Pull the knots to the back and secure the ends with a dot of glue.

supplies

Purchased chambray place mat
  and napkins

Metallic white dimensional
  fabric paint

Small paintbrushes

Super-fine white iridescent glitter

Fabric glue; black seed beads

Scissors; Orange felt scraps;
  narrow red ribbon

Dimensional paint in black, red,
  and green

Needle: Brown perle cotton

confetti cups

Make a plain frosted votive candleholder dance with color. Dip the handle of a paintbrush into glass paint; dab dots at the base of the candleholder to resemble confetti. For the beaded ring, string beads onto elastic thread to make a bracelet the size of the holder top. Knot the elastic ends, trim off the excess, and slip into place. Fill the pretty cup with miniature ornaments for added sparkle.

sweet-as-pie trims

Miniature tart tins form fluted frames for winter scenes snipped from old cards.

1. Using an awl, carefully punch a hole in the top rim of the tart tin.

2. Thread ribbon through the hole, knotting it on the inside of the tin to form a loop for hanging.

3. Trace around the tin onto the card. Using the line as a guide, cut the card slightly smaller to fit inside the tin. Glue the cutout in place with crafts glue.

4. Arrange a ring of miniature artificial fruits or dried flowers around the inside of the tin, gluing it in place with industrial-strength adhesive. Let the adhesive dry.

supplies

Awl

Miniature tart tins

¼-inch-wide ribbon

Greeting cards

Pencil; scissors

Thick white crafts glue

Miniature artificial fruits or
    dried flowers

Industrial-strength adhesive

wintertime coasters

Two favorite Christmastime symbols are permanently etched in glass on these stunning holiday coasters.

supplies

Old greeting cards (for inspiration)

Pencil; paper; crafts knife

Self-adhesive vinyl; scissors

4-inch squares of ¼-inch-thick glass with sanded edges

White vinegar; spoon; etching cream

Black permanent marking pen

White glass paint, such as Liquitex Glossies; small paintbrush

Clear flat marbles or clear adhesive rubber bumper dots; glass cement

1. Using old greeting cards for inspiration, draw a simple design to fit within a 4-inch square. Cut the vinyl into 4-inch squares. Transfer the design to the back of the vinyl. Using a crafts knife, cut out the design.

2. Clean each piece of glass with water and white vinegar. Dry thoroughly. Remove the backing from the vinyl design and place on top of the glass. Rub the back with a spoon to remove air bubbles.

3. Apply etching cream according to the manufacturer's directions. Wash off the cream and remove vinyl. Dry thoroughly.

4. For reindeer, add eyes using black marking pen. For the tree, paint small white dots onto the nonetched side of the coaster.

5. Use cement to apply a flat marble to each corner of the glass, or use adhesive bumpers.

goblet jewelry

Guests will know which drink is theirs with a beautiful beaded ring jingling from the glass stem.

1. Wrap an eye pin around the dowel, allowing the end of the pin to overlap the hoop by ¼ inch. Clip off the excess and bend the end into a hook that will slip through the eye.

2. String beads onto head pins, make a loop at the ends, and slide them onto the ring.

Another Tip or Two

• For sports lovers on your holiday gift list, make goblet jewelry using beads in team colors and sports-themed charms.

• Recycle mismatched earrings by making them into goblet markers.

supplies

4-inch-long eye pin

⁷/₈-inch dowel

Wire cutters

Decorative beads

Head pins

stack of sweetness

Chocolate-peppermint sandwiches, made completely from convenience items, stack up to one sweet and easy-to-make gift.

ingredients

½ cup canned vanilla or
  chocolate frosting

Red and/or green paste food
  coloring (optional)

3 tablespoons finely crushed
  striped round peppermint candies

44 chocolate wafers

Additional crushed candies,
  optional

Round shallow dish to fit cookies

Ribbon

Plastic wrap

Scissors

Prep: 20 minutes Makes: 22 cookie sandwiches

1. In a small mixing bowl stir together frosting, food coloring if desired, and crushed candies.

2. Spread 1 level teaspoon frosting mixture onto each flat side of 22 of the chocolate wafers. Top with the remaining chocolate wafers, flat side toward frosting mixture.

3. Roll edges of cookie sandwiches in additional crushed candies, if desired. Store cookies in airtight container in the refrigerator for up to 3 days.

4. Stack three or four sandwiches, wrap with plastic wrap, and place in a dish. Tie the stack with ribbon to secure. Trim ribbon ends.

candy-filled gifts

Use holiday-shape cookie cutters to hold small sweets.

supplies

Pencil

Open-style cookie cutter
  in desired shape

Lightweight cardboard

Scissors

Clear tape

Nuts or small candies in
  holiday colors

Corsage bag
  (available at floral shops)

8 inches of desired ribbon

1. Draw around the cookie cutter onto the lightweight cardboard. Cut out the shape. Tape the cardboard to the back of the cookie cutter.

2. Fill the cookie cutter with nuts or candies as desired. Leaving cookie cutter laying flat, slide the corsage bag around the cookie cutter and tie a ribbon bow around the open end of the bag.

Another Tip or Two

• Use the candy-filled surprises as package toppers.

• For a student, fill a cookie cutter with quarters for vending machine snacks, laundry, and arcade fun.

canning jar luminaries

For last-minute gifts, fill canning jars with common, yet colorful non-flammable items. Buttons, candy, marbles, and aquarium rocks are some of the items that can be found in holiday red and green. Place a candle in a votive cup and nestle it in the middle of the jar for a glowing effect.

kids' crafts

smiling snow folks

These snappy little fellows with sock-covered faces sport true stocking caps made from the cuffs.

1. Stretch a white sock over a plastic-foam ball. Push the ball into the toe of the sock and cut off the excess, leaving about 3 inches beyond the top of the ball. Using fabric glue, spot-glue the sock in place around the top of the ball.

2. Pull the cuff end of an adult sock over the ball to form the hat, covering the toe seam of the white sock. If desired, turn back the cuff to form a band on the hat. Spot-glue the hat in place. Cut off the remaining sock, leaving 4 to 5 inches beyond the ball for the stocking hat. Tie the top of the hat with yarn to form the shape. Glue or sew on small pom-poms, beads, buttons, jingle bells, or other trims if desired.

3. To create the nose, wrap orange plastic-coated wire around a sharp pencil. Make the nose as long or short as desired. Glue the nose to the face. Glue black sew-on snaps or small black beads to the face for the eyes and mouth.

4. Lightly rub your finger in powdered blush makeup, then rub the blush onto the snowman's face for rosy cheeks. Attach a thin gold wire for hanging.

supplies

Child's white sock, size 4–10

2½-inch plastic-foam ball; scissors

Fabric glue; adult-size patterned
  sock; yarn to match adult sock

Small trims, such as pom-poms,
  beads, buttons, and jingle bells

Orange plastic-coated wire;
  sharp pencil

Black sew-on snaps or small black
  beads; powdered blush makeup

Thin gold wire

swirl-paper ornaments

Hung in a window or on the branches of the tree, your little one's dimensional pretties deserve a place of honor.

supplies

Tracing paper

Pencil

Scissors

Glue stick

Marbled paper

Large safety pin

Fine cord or ribbon

1. Draw a star, tree, bell shape, or other simple shape onto tracing paper; cut out the shape.

2. Rub the glue stick over the back side of one sheet of marbled paper. Press it to the back side of another sheet.

3. Draw around the tracing-paper pattern twice onto the marbled paper and cut out the two shapes.

4. Starting from the bottom of one cutout cut a slit two-thirds of the way up the shape. Using a safety pin, pierce a small hole at the top of the shape; thread a cord or ribbon hanger through the hole, and knot the ends.

5. Starting at the top of the second cutout, cut a slit one-third of the way down. Place the shapes perpendicular to each other, and slip the one with the hanger over the top of the second shape.

tissued treasures

Kids will learn the easy technique of decoupage making these delightful ornaments blanketed with tiny tissue paper squares.

1. Use scissors to cut tissue paper into small squares.

2. Mix a solution of 1 tablespoon water and 1 tablespoon glue in a small dish. Brush a small section of the ornament with the mixture. Use the damp paintbrush to pick up a square of tissue paper and place it onto the wet section of the ornament. Brush a coat of the mixture over the paper. Add paper squares, randomly overlapping and angling papers.

3. After the ball is covered with paper squares, brush on a final coat of the glue and water mixture. If you wish, dust with glitter. Let it dry.

Another Tip or Two

• To give the ornament a more "artsy" feel, tear tissue paper squares instead of cutting them.

• Let every member of the family sign the ornament using colorful permanent marking pens.

supplies

Scissors

Tissue paper in assorted colors

Thick white crafts glue

Water

Small dish

Large round clear glass ornament

Paintbrush

Glitter in desired color(optional)

stained glass ornaments

Your kids will burst with pride when holiday lights shine through their colorful ornaments that resemble those made of leaded glass.

supplies

Holiday-shape cookie cutters

Black crafts foam

Pencil; scissors; plastic wrap; tape

Baking sheet

Broad-tip washable marking pens
  in a variety of colors

Black dimensional paint

Fine black wire

Wire cutters

Thick white crafts glue

1. Place the cookie cutter onto the foam and trace around it. Draw another line $1/4$ inch inside the first line to make a $1/4$-inch frame. Cut along both lines.

2. Tightly tape plastic wrap to a baking sheet. With markers, color the plastic heavily, covering an area slightly larger than the foam frame. Make sure the plastic wrap stays smooth.

3. Run a bead of black dimensional paint around the inner edge of the back of the frame. Press the painted side of the frame onto the colored plastic wrap.

4. Bend a 4-inch length of wire into a U-shape loop for the hanger. Slide the ends of the loop between the frame and plastic, and press the frame over the loop ends.

5. Fill the inside area of the frame with glue. The glue will pick up the marker color as it dries.

6. Let the ornament dry undisturbed for 36 hours or until the color shows through and the glue is almost translucent. Do not touch the glue. Gently peel the ornament from the plastic. If it sticks, let it dry an additional 8 hours. Turn the ornament over and let it dry on a clean piece of plastic for another 8 hours or until dry to the touch.

7. If any glue or black paint leaked from under the frame, trim it off.

child's play

Create playful table accents this holiday season. Let giant snowflakes pause as place mats, build Tinkertoys into a centerpiece tree, and invent place cards using building blocks. Sprinkle the table with tiny toys to delight guests of all ages.

pinecone pots

Use favorite color combinations to make a brilliant parade of miniature holiday trees—the perfect size for small spaces, anywhere in the house.

1. Paint the flowerpots a solid color. Let the paint dry.

2. Choose another color to make stripes or dots. To make stripes, use a flat paintbrush the desired width of the stripe. To make small dots, dip the handle of a paintbrush into paint and dot onto the outside of the pot. For large dots, dip the pencil eraser into paint and dot onto the pot. Let dry.

3. Paint pinecones white. Let the paint dry. Paint them a second time if needed to cover the entire surface white. Let dry.

4. Paint the stars to go with the pots, using coordinating paint colors. Let the paint dry. Dot or stripe the star if you wish. Let dry.

5. Position the pinecone in the pot. If necessary, fill the pot bottom with a piece of crumpled paper napkin so the pinecone sticks out of the top. Place glue in the pot or on the napkin and press the pinecone in place. Glue a star to the top. Let the glue dry.

supplies

1½-inch terra-cotta flowerpots

Acrylic paints in pink,
    orange, purple, blue,
    green, yellow, and white

Paintbrushes, including flat

Pencils

Pinecones

Wood stars

Paper napkins

Thick white crafts glue

totally tubular bracelets

Inexpensive and easy-to-make colorful bracelets come together by the dozens.

supplies

10 inches of clear vinyl tubing, available at hardware stores

1 inch of clear vinyl tubing just small enough to fit snugly inside the first tubing

Small funnel to fit inside the long tubing (optional)

Bracelet filler such as seed beads, other small beads, glitter, and multicolor chenille strips

1. Wrap the 10-inch piece of tubing around your wrist to check for fit. Make sure it can slip over your hand. Trim the tubing to the proper length.

2. Slide the small tube halfway into one end of the larger tube. This will be the connector that joins the tube ends into a bracelet.

3. To fill the bracelet with beads or glitter, hold one finger over the end of the small connector. Use a funnel to fill the large tube with glitter or beads, mixing or arranging colors as desired.

4. To fill the bracelet with chenille strips, choose two to four chenille strips in coordinating colors. Twist the strips together, keeping the ends even. Slide the twisted strips into the tube until they reach the connector. Trim the stems 1 inch longer than the large tube.

5. Wrap the tube into a circle. For the chenille bracelet, slide the ends of the chenille into the connector. For all bracelets, slide the large end of the tube over the remaining end of the connector so the bracelet fits tightly together.

feather angels

These soft feather angels are so heavenly to craft, kids will want to make one for every member of the family.

1. Use scissors to cut off the tip of the paper cup.

2. Spread glue on half of the outside of the cone. Choose feathers that look pretty together. Place the feathers onto the glue, facing all the feathers in the same direction with the wide ends pointing downward. When the first half is done, cover the other cone half with glue and feathers.

3. For wings, glue large feathers onto the back.

4. Wrap one end of the chenille stem tightly around a pencil four times. Remove it from the pencil. Push the straight end of the chenille stem through the bead down to where it curls. Push the chenille stem into the tip of the cone and tape it in place onto the inside of the cone.

supplies

Scissors

Paper cone cups, available
    at bottled-water companies

Thick white crafts glue

Colorful feathers, available
    at crafts stores

Metallic gold chenille stems

Pencil

Large colored wood bead

Tape

peppermint temptations

Gift recipients will praise these minty sensations made from the perfect pair of white chocolate and peppermint.

ingredients

1 pound white chocolate baking pieces or vanilla-flavored candy coating, cut up

$1/3$ cup finely crushed peppermint candy

2 tablespoons coarsely crushed peppermint candy

Prep: 25 minutes Chill: 30 minutes Makes: about $1^1/4$ pounds

1. Line a baking sheet with foil; set aside.

2. Heat baking pieces or candy coating in a heavy 2-quart saucepan over low heat, stirring constantly until melted and smooth. Remove from heat. Stir in $1/3$ cup finely crushed peppermint candy.

3. Pour mixture onto the prepared baking sheet, spreading to about a 10-inch circle. Sprinkle with 2 tablespoons crushed peppermint candy. Chill about 30 minutes or until firm.

4. Use the foil to lift candy from the baking sheet; break candy into pieces. Store, tightly covered, in the refrigerator.

Another Tip or Two

• Use decorative tins or boxes to package the candy. If desired, paint a plain round cardboard container with white and red stripes to resemble a peppermint candy.

• Wrap the container in clear plastic wrap and tie the ends with ribbon to look like a giant piece of candy.

candy canes for claus

Surprise Santa with tasty treats on his cookie plate this Christmas.

1. Thread four jingle bells onto a chenille stem. Space the bells so one is near each end and two are in the middle.

2. Carefully wrap the chenille stem around the candy cane. Glue the chenille stem ends to the candy cane and let dry.

Another Tip or Two

• Thread a holiday message onto the chenille stem using large-hole alphabet beads.

• Look for multicolor candy canes and jingle bells to make brighter versions of this project.

supplies

Jingle bells in metallic red,
   gold, and green

Red metallic chenille stems

Candy canes in wrappers in
   desired colors

Thick white crafts glue

holiday snowmen

Enjoy a cozy wintry afternoon with the kids making, decorating, and eating these whimsical cookies.

ingredients

18-ounce roll refrigerated
   chocolate chip, sugar, or peanut
   butter cookie dough

1 cup sifted powdered sugar

$1/4$ teaspoon vanilla

1 to 2 tablespoons milk

Gumdrops

Miniature semisweet
   chocolate pieces

Prep: 20 minutes Bake: 8 minutes per batch
Oven: 375°F Makes: 18 cookies

1. Cut cookie dough into 18 equal pieces. Divide each dough piece into three balls: one large (about $1^1/4$ inches in diameter), one medium (about 1 inch in diameter), and one small (about $3/4$ inch in diameter). Assemble each set of balls $1/4$ inch apart in a snowman shape on an ungreased cookie sheet, placing the largest balls 2 inches apart so the snowmen don't bake together.

2. Bake in a 375° oven for 8 to 10 minutes or until edges are very lightly browned. Cool on cookie sheet for 3 minutes. Transfer cookies to a wire rack and let cool.

3. For glaze, in a small bowl stir together powdered sugar, vanilla, and 1 tablespoon milk. Stir in additional milk, 1 teaspoon at a time, to make glaze of drizzling consistency. Spoon glaze over snowmen. Decorate as desired with gumdrops and/or chocolate pieces.

terrific tins

Even after the edibles are gone, friends and family can continue to enjoy your child's handiwork on personalized tins.

supplies

Newspapers; cookie tins

Spray primer

Acrylic paint in blue, purple,
   green, white, orange, and black

2 circular sponges; scissors

Felt in orange and yellow; thick
   white crafts glue; small pom-pom

Small twigs; ribbon; 2 buttons

Snowflake rubber stamp;
   spray clear coat high-shine glaze

Cotton swabs

Here's how to make the snowman tin

1. In a well-ventilated work area, cover the work surface with newspapers. Spray the tin with primer and let dry. Paint two coats of blue paint onto the tin; let dry between coats. Sponge on purple; let dry. Onto lid, sponge two white circles for snowman; let dry.

2. Cut out an orange felt triangle for the hat and a yellow strip for the hatband; glue to tin. Glue pom-pom at the tip of the hat. Glue on twigs for arms and ribbon for a scarf. Glue buttons onto the center of the large white circle. Let dry. Paint eyes, a mouth, and an orange carrot nose onto the small circle. Stamp snowflakes around the side of the tin. Let dry.

3. In a well-ventilated work area, spray the lid and base separately with clear coat. Let dry.

Here's how to make the handprint tin

1. In a well-ventilated work area, cover the work surface with newspapers. Spray the tin with primer and let dry. Paint the tin a dark color and sponge on a light color as for the snowman tin.

2. Coat child's hand with contrasting paint and press onto the lid. Use a cotton swab to make a border of small dots around the edge. Press thumbprints onto the side rim. Let dry. Finish as in Step 3, above.

snow bowls

Use little dabs of ceramic paint to turn white soup or chili bowls into cheery servers.

1. Wash and dry the bowls thoroughly. Using paints, paint black dots for the eyes, black Xs for the mouth, and black squiggles for the eyebrows. Add an orange triangular nose, tipping or curving it slightly.

2. Dip your finger into red paint, blot off the excess onto a paper towel, and rub cheeks onto the face. Let the paint dry. Cure the paint according to the manufacturer's directions.

3. Twist two chenille stems together for the handle. Glue the handle ends in place on either side of the bowl and let dry. Glue a matching pom-pom over each chenille stem end. Let the glue dry. **Note:** The chenille and pom pom ear muffs are for decoration only. Avoid carrying the bowl by this "handle" to prevent breaking and spilling.

4. Wrap a wool strip around the bowl, tie it, and tack it to the bowl base with glue. Trim and fringe the ends as desired. Glue or sew buttons down the center of the scarf.

supplies

White soup or chili bowls

Paints for ceramics or glass in black, orange, and red

Paintbrush; paper towel

Chenille stems in desired colors

Strong adhesive, such as E6000

1-inch-diameter pom-poms

4×36-inch strips of wool

Buttons

Needle and thread (optional)

glistening ice rings

Treat your backyard birds to one-of-a-kind ice rings filled with scrumptious berries and seeds.

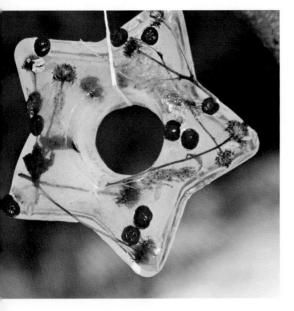

supplies

Gelatin ring molds or mini
  aluminum pie tins

Plastic disposable cups

Water

Cranberries

Sticks

Birdseed

String

1. Use a ring mold or place a plastic cup into the center of the pie tin. If using a cup, put some water in it so it does not float in the pie tin. Fill the mold or pie tin halfway with water.

2. Arrange the cranberries, sticks, and birdseed in the water. Let the ring freeze until solid.

3. To remove the ring from the mold, run cold water over the back of the ring. Remove the cup.

4. Tie or loop string around the ring and hang in a tree or bush. To make the ice rings last the longest, hang them in the shade during your coldest weather.

mini treasure chests

Petite boxes are perfect for presenting tiny tokens to teachers and friends.

1. Using the paintbrush, apply two coats of red, green, white, or metallic gold paint to the outside of each box and lid, letting the paint dry between coats.

2. Glue the dry pasta to the box top, arranging as you wish. Let dry.

3. Apply a light coat of gold glitter paint to the entire box, including the pasta. Let dry.

Another Tip or Two

• If you can't find tree-shape pasta, use bow-tie pasta or tiny stars.

• Place holiday words or someone's name on the box lid using alphabet macaroni. To make gluing easier, dip a toothpick in glue and dot where the pasta piece is desired onto the box lid.

supplies

Foam paintbrush

Acrylic paint in red, green, white, metallic gold, and gold glitter

Small papier-mâché boxes in graduated sizes

Thick white crafts glue

Christmas-tree-shape pasta

gathering together

spiral-sliced ham with two simple sauces

For added flavor and variety serve one or both sauces with your holiday ham. Each can be made in advance and refrigerated up to 24 hours ahead.

Prep: 10 minutes Bake: 2 hours Stand: 20 minutes
Oven: 300°F Makes: 12 to 16 servings

1. Place ham into a roasting pan according to package directions (discard flavor or seasoning packet). Roast in a 300° oven about 2 hours or until thermometer registers 140°F.

2. Meanwhile, prepare sauces. Remove ham from oven; cover with foil and let stand for 20 minutes before serving. Pass sauces with ham.

Dried Cherry Chutney: Place ³/₄ cup dried cherries and ¹/₂ cup coarsely snipped dried apricots into a bowl; cover with boiling water. Let stand for 5 minutes. Drain; transfer fruit to a food processor. Add 3 sliced green onions. Cover and process with on/off turns until chopped. (If you don't have a food processor, finely chop the cherries, apricots, and green onions with a knife.) In a small saucepan heat 3 tablespoons red jalapeño jelly over medium-low heat just until melted; stir in chopped fruit mixture and ¹/₄ cup finely chopped toasted pecans. Makes 1¹/₃ cups.

Plum-Mustard Sauce: In a small saucepan heat an 18-ounce jar of red plum jam (1¹/₂ cups) over medium-low heat until jam is melted and bubbly. Stir in 2 tablespoons honey mustard and ¹/₈ teaspoon black pepper. Serve warm. Makes about 1¹/₂ cups.

ingredients

1 7- to 8-pound cooked spiral-sliced ham

Dried Cherry Chutney

Plum-Mustard Sauce

volcano potatoes

Your grandmother made gravy—you're the expert on gourmet potatoes. Both are memorable, but yours take a lot less time.

Prep: 15 minutes Bake: 65 minutes

Oven: 300°F/375°F Makes: 10 servings

1. Place potatoes in a 2-quart baking dish. Bake, covered, in a 300° oven for 50 minutes.

2. Meanwhile, in a medium mixing bowl beat the whipping cream with an electric mixer on medium speed until soft peaks form (tips curl). Fold in the cheese.

3. Increase oven temperature to 375°. Remove dish from oven; uncover. With a large spoon push potatoes from the center to the sides making a hole. Spoon the whipping cream mixture into the hole. Sprinkle top with cracked black pepper.

4. Bake, uncovered, for 15 to 20 minutes more or until top is golden.

ingredients

3   20-ounce packages refrigerated mashed potatoes

¾   cup whipping cream

1   cup shredded Gruyère, Havarti, or American cheese (4 ounces)

Freshly cracked black pepper

vegetable medley au gratin

No peeling or chopping the vegetables! An easy-to-use bag of frozen vegetables goes gourmet with a buttery walnut topping.

Prep: 20 minutes Bake: 65 minutes

Oven: 300°F/375°F Makes: 10 servings

1. In a large bowl combine soup, sour cream, and dill. Stir in thawed vegetables. Transfer to a 2-quart rectangular baking dish.

2. Bake, covered, in a 300° oven for 50 minutes. In a small bowl combine crackers, walnuts, Parmesan cheese, and melted butter. Uncover baking dish and sprinkle vegetable mixture with crumb mixture. Increase oven temperature to 375°. Bake casserole, uncovered, about 15 minutes more or until topping is browned.

Make-Ahead Tip: Prepare, cover, and chill vegetable and crumb mixtures separately overnight before baking.

ingredients

1 $10^3/_4$-ounce can condensed cream of chicken and mushroom soup

$^1/_2$ cup dairy sour cream

$^1/_2$ teaspoon dried dill

2 16-ounce packages loose-pack frozen broccoli, cauliflower, and carrots, thawed

$^2/_3$ cup crushed stone-ground wheat crackers (about 15 crackers)

$^1/_3$ cup finely chopped walnuts

$^1/_4$ cup shredded Parmesan cheese

2 tablespoons butter, melted

maple orange–glazed turkey roast

If you prefer to rinse your turkey, use hot soapy water to clean all surfaces that come in contact with the raw turkey and its juices.

ingredients

½   teaspoon bottled garlic (1 clove)

1   tablespoon snipped fresh marjoram or 1 teaspoon dried marjoram, crushed

¼   teaspoon salt

¼   teaspoon black pepper

¾   cup orange juice

1   tablespoon cornstarch

½   cup pure maple syrup

1   teaspoon finely shredded orange peel

1   2½- to 3½-pound boneless turkey roast

2   tablespoons butter, melted

Prep: 20 minutes Grill: 2 hours
Stand: 15 minutes Makes: 10 to 12 servings

1. In a small bowl combine garlic, marjoram, salt, and pepper; set aside. For glaze, in a small saucepan stir together orange juice and cornstarch; add half of the garlic mixture. Cook and stir over medium heat until thickened and bubbly. Cook and stir for 1 minute more. Stir in maple syrup and orange peel; set aside.

2. Brush the turkey roast with melted butter. Sprinkle remaining garlic mixture evenly over turkey roast; rub in with your fingers. Insert an oven-going meat thermometer near the center of the turkey roast.

3. For a charcoal grill, arrange medium-hot coals around a drip pan. Test for medium heat above the pan. Place the turkey roast directly onto the grill rack over the pan. Cover; grill for 2 to 2½ hours or until thermometer registers 165°F. Add coals to maintain heat every 30 minutes. Brush with glaze frequently during the last 30 minutes of grilling. (For a gas grill, preheat grill. Reduce heat to medium. Adjust for indirect cooking. Grill as above.)

4. Remove turkey from grill. Cover with foil; let stand for 15 minutes before carving. (The turkey's temperature will rise 5°F during standing.) Bring any remaining glaze to boiling; pass with turkey.

bistro beef and mushrooms

Many American bistros look to France for inspiration, serving meals with classic French flair. This simple dish taps into Burgundy with Dijon mustard, red wine, and thyme.

Start to Finish: 25 minutes Makes: 4 servings

1. Spread mustard evenly over both sides of steaks. Season steaks with salt and pepper. In a large skillet cook steaks over medium-high heat in 1 tablespoon hot oil until desired doneness, turning once. Allow 7 to 9 minutes for medium rare (145°F) and 10 to 12 minutes for medium (160°F). Transfer steaks to a serving platter; keep warm.

2. Add the remaining 1 tablespoon oil to drippings in skillet. Cook and stir mushrooms in hot oil over medium-high heat for 4 minutes. Carefully stir in wine, Worcestershire sauce, and thyme. Cook and stir about 3 minutes more or until mushroom mixture is reduced to desired consistency. Season to taste with salt and pepper. Spoon over steaks.

*Note: Crimini or portobello mushrooms would work in this dish as well.

ingredients

1　tablespoon Dijon-style mustard or coarse-grain brown mustard

4　4- to 5-ounce beef tenderloin steaks, $3/4$ inch thick

　Salt and black pepper

2　tablespoons olive oil or cooking oil

1　8-ounce package sliced button mushrooms (about 3 cups)*

$1/3$　cup dry red wine or beef broth

1　tablespoon white wine Worcestershire sauce

2　teaspoons snipped fresh thyme

cherry tomatoes stuffed with herbed cheese

Prepare these tiny bright bite-size gems up to two hours in advance, then cover and refrigerate until serving time.

Start to Finish: 25 minutes Makes: 36 stuffed tomatoes

1. Using a sharp knife cut off the top one-third of each tomato. Set aside the tops for garnish, if desired, or discard. Hollow out tomatoes; invert onto paper towels to drain and set aside.

2. Place pesto, garlic, the 2 tablespoons parsley, the chives, and tarragon in a food processor; process for 15 seconds. Add the cream cheese and chèvre; process another 30 to 45 seconds or until smooth.

3. Place cheese mixture into a pastry bag fitted with a star tip and pipe into cherry tomatoes. If desired, garnish with fresh parsley or dill sprigs and/or reserved tomato tops.

ingredients

3 dozen cherry tomatoes, 1 to 1½ inches in diameter

2 tablespoons purchased pesto

1 clove garlic, minced

2 tablespoons snipped fresh parsley

2 tablespoons snipped fresh chives

1 tablespoon snipped fresh tarragon or dill

1 8-ounce package cream cheese

4 ounces goat cheese (chèvre) or cream cheese

Fresh parsley or fresh dill sprigs (optional)

parmigiana cheesecake with pears

Recognize real Parmigiana—imported from Italy—by the name stamped on the rind and its spectacularly rich, nutty taste. *Pictured on page 128.*

ingredients

¼ cup crisp rye cracker crumbs

6¼ cups freshly grated Parmigiana-Reggiano cheese

1 tablespoon butter, melted

4 8-ounce packages cream cheese, softened

½ cup whipping cream

4 eggs

½ cup shredded Gruyère cheese

⅓ cup snipped fresh chives

¼ teaspoon cracked white peppercorns

Fresh Asian pears or other pears, cored, cut into wedges, and tossed in 2 teaspoons lemon juice

Prep: 30 minutes Bake: 1 hour 45 minutes Cool: 45 minutes
Oven: 300°F Makes: 25 to 30 servings

1. For crust, combine cracker crumbs, ¼ cup of the Parmigiana-Reggiano cheese, and the melted butter. Sprinkle 3 tablespoons of the crumb mixture into a generously buttered 9-inch springform pan, lightly dusting the sides and bottom of pan. Refrigerate the remaining crumbs until ready to use.

2. In a large mixing bowl beat cream cheese and whipping cream with an electric mixer on medium speed just until smooth. Add eggs, beating until just combined. Stir in the remaining 6 cups Parmigiana-Reggiano cheese, the Gruyère cheese, chives, and peppercorns with a rubber spatula until smooth. Pour mixture into prepared pan, spreading evenly. Sprinkle reserved crumb mixture over top.

3. Set springform pan onto a cookie sheet. Bake in a 300° oven for 1 hour 45 minutes. Transfer to a wire rack and let cool in pan for 15 minutes. Loosen the cheesecake from sides of pan and cool for 30 minutes more. (Center may dip slightly as it cools.)

4. To serve, warm the blade of a serrated knife under hot running water and cut cheesecake into wedges. Rewarm blade after each cut. Serve cheesecake as spread with pear wedges.

crab mousse in cucumbers

Vary the recipe with cooked smoked salmon or whitefish instead of the crab. *Pictured on page 128.*

Start to Finish: 30 minutes Makes: about 40 pieces

1. Remove 2 tablespoons crabmeat for garnish, if desired. Place remaining crabmeat, the cream cheese, mayonnaise, mustard, shallot, horseradish, red pepper, and if desired, salt into a food processor. Cover and process until smooth, scraping sides of bowl. Spoon mixture into a pastry bag fitted with a large star tip.

2. Using a zester or vegetable peeler, peel the cucumbers, leaving some strips of skin. Cut into 3/4-inch-thick slices. (Or halve 2 cucumbers lengthwise and slice 3/4 inch thick.) With a melon baller, scoop out the center of each slice to create a cup. Pipe mousse into cucumber cups. Sprinkle each with reserved crabmeat, if desired. Serve immediately or cover and chill up to 2 hours before serving.

ingredients

1/2 pound flaked cooked crabmeat or flake-style imitation crabmeat

1 3-ounce package cream cheese, cut up and softened

2 tablespoons mayonnaise

1 tablespoon Dijon-style mustard

1 tablespoon finely chopped shallot

2 teaspoons prepared horseradish

1/2 teaspoon ground red pepper

1/4 teaspoon salt (optional)

4 medium cucumbers, each about 8 inches long

orange martini shrimp cocktail

Serve this enticing appetizer in martini glasses for a festive presentation.

Prep: 15 minutes Chill: 2 hours Makes: 6 servings

1. Thaw shrimp, if frozen. Peel and devein shrimp, leaving tails intact. Cook shrimp in lightly salted boiling water for 2 to 3 minutes or until shrimp turn opaque, stirring occasionally; drain. Rinse in a colander under cold running water; drain. Place shrimp into a plastic bag set in a medium bowl; set aside.

2. In a small bowl combine vodka, oil, mint, and orange peel. Pour mixture over shrimp; seal bag. Marinate in the refrigerator for 2 to 4 hours, turning bag occasionally.

3. To serve, place about 1/3 cup crushed ice into each of six chilled martini glasses or small serving bowls. Drain shrimp; discard marinade. Arrange shrimp in each glass on top of ice. Garnish with orange peel twists. If desired, drizzle each with 1 to 2 teaspoons vermouth.

*Note: If you can't find orange-flavored vodka in local stores, use 1/4 cup plain vodka and 2 tablespoons orange juice.

ingredients

18   fresh or frozen jumbo shrimp
       in shells (about 1 pound)

1/3   cup orange-flavored vodka

1   tablespoon cooking oil

1   tablespoon snipped fresh mint

1   teaspoon finely shredded
       orange peel

      Crushed ice

      Orange peel twists

      Dry vermouth (optional)

smoked salmon mousse

Salmon mousse is always an impressive appetizer, but when you use smoked salmon instead of regular canned salmon, it becomes downright unbelievable.

Prep: 45 minutes Chill: 4½ hours Makes: 16 servings

1. Place water in a saucepan. Sprinkle unflavored gelatin and sugar over the water; let stand for 3 minutes to soften gelatin. Heat, stirring constantly, over medium heat until gelatin dissolves. Remove from heat.

2. In a large bowl combine mayonnaise, tomato sauce, lemon juice, dried dill, and pepper; stir in gelatin mixture. Chill until partially set, about 30 minutes. Fold in salmon, celery, chopped eggs, and chives.

3. In a small mixing bowl beat whipping cream with an electric mixer on medium speed until soft peaks form (tips curl). Fold whipped cream into salmon mixture. Pour into a 6-cup fish-shaped or ring mold. Cover and chill until firm, about 4 hours. To serve, line a tray or serving plate with lettuce, if desired. Unmold mousse onto tray. Garnish with cucumber slices and fresh dill. Serve with assorted crackers.

Unmolding: Set the mold in a bowl or sink filled with warm water for several seconds or until the edges appear to pull away from the mold.

*Note: To make hard-cooked eggs, place eggs in a saucepan. Add enough cold water to just cover the eggs. Bring to a rapid boil over high heat. Remove from heat, cover, and let stand 15 minutes; drain. Run cold water over the eggs or place them in ice water until cool enough to handle; drain. To peel eggs, gently tap each egg on the countertop. Roll the egg between the palms of your hands. Peel off eggshell, starting at the large end.

ingredients

¾   cup water

2   envelopes unflavored gelatin

1   teaspoon sugar

1¼ cups mayonnaise or salad
    dressing

¼   cup tomato sauce

¼   cup lemon juice

1   teaspoon dried dill

¼   teaspoon black pepper

1   pound smoked salmon,
    flaked, with skin and
    bones removed

½   cup chopped celery (1 stalk)

2   hard-cooked eggs*, chopped

2   tablespoons snipped
    fresh chives

¾   cup whipping cream

    Lettuce (optional)

    Thin cucumber slices

    Fresh dill

    Assorted crackers and/or
    baguette slices

gorgonzola and walnut terrine with apples

Add this cheery, cheesy appetizer to your holiday spread, and guests will linger around the table for double helpings.

Prep: 15 minutes Bake: 8 minutes Oven: 350°F Chill: overnight
Makes: 12 to 16 servings Stand: 30 minutes

1. Spread walnuts onto a baking sheet; toast in a 350° oven about 8 minutes or until lightly browned and fragrant, stirring once. Let cool.

2. Line a 5$\frac{1}{2}$×3×2-inch loaf pan with plastic wrap, extending 3 inches of wrap over the pan edges. In a large bowl, break up the cheese with a fork until slightly chunky. Add walnuts and sour cream; mix thoroughly. Spoon mixture into the loaf pan and spread evenly. Cover with the overhanging plastic wrap; refrigerate overnight or until very firm.

3. Let terrine stand at room temperature for 30 minutes before serving. To serve, unfold the plastic and turn the terrine out onto a platter lined with lettuce leaves. Discard plastic wrap. Core and slice the apples into wedges. Cut the baguette into $\frac{1}{2}$-inch slices. Arrange apple and baguette slices alongside terrine.

ingredients

1   cup walnuts, finely chopped
    (about 4 ounces)

$\frac{1}{2}$ pound Gorgonzola or blue
    cheese, room temperature

$\frac{1}{2}$ cup dairy sour cream

    Lettuce leaves

    Fuji or Granny Smith apples

    Sourdough baguette

mapled brie and apples

The "Brie bake" rises to any special occasion when enhanced with maple syrup and spiked with spirits for extra flavor.

Prep: 20 minutes Bake: 21 minutes
Oven: 425°F/350°F Makes: 20 servings

1. Prepare Cinnamon Crostini. Reduce oven temperature to 350°. Place Brie onto an ovenproof platter. Bake about 15 minutes or until warm and soft but not runny. (Or place Brie on a microwave-safe platter and microwave, uncovered, on 100 percent power [high] about 40 seconds.)

2. Meanwhile, in a small saucepan combine brown sugar, maple syrup, and brandy. Bring to boiling, stirring to dissolve sugar. Reduce heat; simmer, uncovered, about 5 minutes or until slightly thickened. Stir in walnuts. Pour over softened Brie. Serve immediately with Cinnamon Crostini and apple slices.

Make-Ahead Tip: Make the Cinnamon Crostini the day before and store it in a covered container.

Cinnamon Crostini: Cut twenty 1/2-inch diagonal slices from an 8-ounce French bread baguette. Brush one side of slices evenly with 3 tablespoons melted butter. Sprinkle with cinnamon sugar or maple sugar. Arrange on an ungreased baking sheet. Bake in a 425°F oven for 6 to 8 minutes or until crisp and light brown.

ingredients

Cinnamon Crostini

1 8-ounce round Brie cheese

3 tablespoons packed brown sugar

3 tablespoons maple syrup

3 tablespoons brandy

1/4 cup chopped walnuts, toasted

2 apples, cored and thinly sliced

wrap-and-roll basil pinwheels

These super-easy, yet very impressive appetizers will be a hit at your next holiday gathering. No one has to know how simple they really are to make.

Prep: 20 minutes Chill: 2 hours Makes: 18 to 20 slices

1. Spread each tortilla evenly with some of the cheese (if cheese seems crumbly, stir it until smooth). Cover cheese layer with large basil leaves. Arrange roasted red pepper strips over basil leaves. Top with meat slices. Tightly roll up each tortilla into a spiral, tucking in meat as you roll. Wrap each roll in plastic wrap. Chill rolls in the refrigerator for 2 to 4 hours.

2. To serve, remove plastic wrap from rolls. Trim ends of rolls; cut rolls into 1-inch-thick slices. Skewer each slice onto a pick or short decorative skewer, if desired. Arrange slices on a platter. If desired, garnish platter with additional fresh basil leaves.

ingredients

3 7- or 8-inch flour tortillas

1 5.2-ounce container semisoft cheese with garlic and herbs

12 large fresh basil leaves

½ 7-ounce jar (⅔ cup) roasted red sweet peppers, cut into thin strips

4 ounces thinly sliced cooked ham, roast beef, or turkey

   Fresh basil leaves (optional)

hot artichoke and roasted pepper dip

Traditional artichoke dip gets a twist from leeks and roasted red peppers. For a pretty presentation, serve with red, green, and yellow sweet peppers for dipping.

Prep: 20 minutes Bake: 20 minutes Oven: 350°F Makes: 3 cups

1. In a medium skillet cook leek in hot butter over medium heat until tender. Remove from heat. Stir in artichoke hearts, roasted red peppers, the 1 cup Parmesan cheese, the mayonnaise, sour cream, and black pepper.

2. Spread mixture evenly into an 8-inch quiche dish or 9-inch pie plate. Sprinkle with the 2 tablespoons Parmesan cheese and the parsley. If desired, cover and chill up to 24 hours before baking.

3. Bake, uncovered, in a 350° oven about 20 minutes or until heated through. Serve with sweet pepper wedges, pita bread, or bagel crisps.

1   medium leek, quartered lengthwise and thinly sliced, or $1/3$ cup sliced green onions (about 3)

2   teaspoons butter

1   14-ounce can artichoke hearts, drained and coarsely chopped

1   7-ounce jar roasted red sweet peppers, drained and coarsely chopped

1   cup grated Parmesan cheese

$1/2$ cup mayonnaise

$1/2$ cup dairy sour cream

$1/8$ teaspoon black pepper

2   tablespoons grated Parmesan cheese

1   tablespoon snipped fresh parsley

Assorted sweet pepper wedges, pita bread, or bagel crisps

cranberry vodka

The vodka takes on a transparent pink blush as it mingles with the berries.

Prep: 10 minutes Stand: 2 weeks Makes: 16 (1-ounce) servings

1. Wash cranberries; pat dry. Place cranberries into a clean 1-quart jar. Pour vodka over fruit. Cover jar tightly with a nonmetallic lid (or cover jar with plastic wrap and tightly seal with a metal lid). Let stand in a cool, dark place for 2 weeks. (Keeps up to 2 months.)

2. To serve, pour vodka and some of the cranberries into small glasses. If desired, garnish with lemon slices.

ingredients

2 cups cranberries

2 cups vodka

Lemon slices (optional)

cranberry-orange martini

Be sure to use top quality liqueurs for this delicious party drink.

Start to Finish: 5 minutes Makes: 1 serving

1. In a cocktail shaker combine cranberry juice, vodka, orange liqueur, and ice. Cover and shake. Strain mixture into a chilled martini glass. If desired, garnish with a cherry and chopped papaya or mango.

ingredients

2 tablespoons cranberry juice

2 tablespoons vodka

2 tablespoons orange-flavored liqueur

Ice cubes

Maraschino cherry (optional)

Finely chopped papaya or mango (optional)

CHRISTMAS SWEETS & TREATS **139**

hot gingered cider

A cupful of this spicy drink just might be the answer after a day of sledding or hitting the slopes.

ingredients

1   1-liter bottle ginger ale

4   cups apple cider

¼   cup mulling spices

2   tablespoons lemon juice

1   1-inch piece fresh ginger,
     peeled and sliced

Prep: 10 minutes Cook: about 20 minutes Makes: 8 to 10 servings

1. In a large saucepan combine ginger ale, apple cider, mulling spices, lemon juice, and fresh ginger. Cover and heat over medium-low heat about 20 minutes or until heated through (do not boil). Strain and discard the spices.

2. To serve, ladle cider into heatproof glass mugs or cups.

hot apple cider with calvados

Calvados is an apple brandy produced in northern France.

ingredients

1   gallon apple cider

1   cup strong-brewed tea

4   3-inch cinnamon sticks

1   cup Calvados or apple brandy

    Cinnamon sticks

    Crab apples (optional)

Prep: 10 minutes Cook: 20 minutes Makes: 16 to 20 servings

1. In a 6- to 8-quart Dutch oven combine apple cider, tea, and 4 cinnamon sticks. Bring just to a simmer (do not boil). Simmer, uncovered, for 20 minutes. Remove cinnamon sticks. Stir in Calvados.

2. To serve, pour into porcelain or heatproof glass mugs, and garnish each with a cinnamon stick and if desired, a crab apple.

timberline hot chocolate

Schlag is a German word used mainly in Austria for whipped cream.

Start to Finish: 20 minutes Makes: 4 to 6 servings

1. In a medium saucepan combine milk, water, and sugar. Stir over medium heat until mixture just comes to boiling. Remove from heat. Stir in chocolate. Beat with an immersion blender, rotary mixer, or whisk until chocolate is melted and mixture is frothy.

2. To serve, pour hot chocolate into cups. If desired, top with Schlag, crushed English toffee, and cocoa powder.

Schlag: In a medium mixing bowl combine 1 cup whipping cream, 2 tablespoons sugar, and 2 teaspoons vanilla. Beat with an electric mixer on medium speed until soft peaks form (tips curl).

ingredients

4 cups milk

$1/2$ cup water

$1/2$ cup sugar

8 ounces bittersweet or semisweet chocolate, coarsely chopped

Schlag (optional)

English toffee, crushed (optional)

Unsweetened cocoa powder (optional)

sweeten the scene

special sugar cookie cutouts

Use as many colors of dough as you like—the decorating's done on these before they go into the oven! For a classic sugar cookie, leave out the food coloring.

Prep: 35 minutes Chill: 1¼ hours Bake: 7 minutes per batch
Oven: 375°F Makes: 48 (2½-inch) cookies or 16 (5¼-inch) cookies

1. In a medium mixing bowl beat butter and shortening with an electric mixer on medium to high speed for 30 seconds. Add sugar, baking powder, and salt. Beat until combined, scraping sides of bowl occasionally. Beat in egg and vanilla. Beat in as much of the flour as you can with the mixer. Stir in any remaining flour.

2. Divide dough into portions, tinting each portion with a different color of food coloring, kneading until dough is evenly colored. Cover; chill about 1 hour or until dough is easy to handle.

3. On a lightly floured surface, roll one portion of the dough at a time until ⅛ inch thick. Using 2½-inch cookie cutters, cut out dough into desired shapes. (For 5¼-inch cookies, roll dough to ¼-inch thickness.) Place cutouts on an ungreased cookie sheet. Refrigerate cutouts for 15 minutes. Using small cookie cutters, make smaller cutouts and fill each opening with another color of dough.

4. Bake in a 375° oven for 7 to 8 minutes for smaller cookies or about 10 minutes for larger cookies, or until edges are firm and bottoms are very lightly browned. Cool 2 minutes on cookie sheet. Transfer to a wire rack and let cool.

ingredients

⅓ cup butter, softened

⅓ cup shortening

¾ cup sugar

1 teaspoon baking powder

  Dash salt

1 egg

1 teaspoon vanilla

2 cups all-purpose flour

  Paste food coloring

gingerbread cookie dough

What could be cozier this time of year than a cute little log cabin in the woods dusted with sparkling, sugary snow?

Prep: 30 minutes Bake: 8 minutes per batch Oven: 375°F

1. In a mixing bowl beat shortening with an electric mixer on medium speed for 30 seconds. Beat in sugar, ginger, cinnamon, and cloves until combined, scraping bowl occasionally. Beat in egg, molasses, corn syrup, and water. Beat in as much of the flour as you can with the mixer. Stir in any remaining flour.

2. On a lightly floured surface, shape dough into ½-inch diameter ropes. Cut ropes into nine 9-inch logs, fourteen 7-inch logs, seven 3-inch logs, seven 4-inch logs, and twelve 1½-inch logs. Place logs onto ungreased baking sheet. With your finger, make a depression ½ inch from each end on all logs, except the 1½-inch logs. On the 1½-inch logs, make depression only in the center. Reshape the depressions slightly to keep logs an even width. Bake in a 375° oven for 8 minutes. Cool for 1 minute on baking sheet . Transfer to a wire rack; cool completely.

3. Enlarge the roof, roof base, and gable pattern pieces on page 155 as directed. If desired, laminate pattern pieces to protect them. Prepare a second batch of dough. Roll out dough onto the back of an ungreased 15×10×1-inch baking pan or flat baking sheet to ⅛ to ¼ inch thick. (If desired, place pan or baking sheet onto a damp towel to prevent it from sliding around.) Place pattern pieces 1 inch apart on dough. Cut around patterns with a sharp knife. Remove excess dough. Bake in a 375° oven about 8 minutes or until edges are brown and dough is firm. Cool for 1 minute on pan. Loosen bottoms of baked pieces with a spatula. Cool completely on pan.

ingredients

- 1 cup shortening
- 1 cup sugar
- 1 teaspoon ground ginger
- ¾ teaspoon ground cinnamon
- ½ teaspoon ground cloves
- 1 egg
- ½ cup molasses
- ⅓ cup light-colored corn syrup
- 1 tablespoon water
- 5 cups all-purpose flour

gingerbread log cabin decorating and assembling

decorations

Royal Icing (see recipe, page 40)

Cinnamon graham cracker rectangles

Mixed nuts

Wheat wafers

Breadsticks

Paste food coloring

Small candies for decorating

Powdered sugar (optional)

Assemble and display the log cabin on a large cutting board. Pipe Royal Icing from a pastry bag fitted with a small star tip, or spread icing to fasten pieces together. Experiment to find the right amount of icing to use. If you apply too little icing, the pieces won't stay together, yet too much icing takes too long to dry. Let each set of pieces stand about 1 hour or until the icing is dry before continuing.

Attach gables to roof base (see illustration, opposite middle). Use custard cups to secure the gables while icing dries. Attach back roof to gables; set the front roof aside to attach later.

Assemble the log cabin walls using 9-inch logs for the back, 7-inch logs for the sides, 3- and 4-inch logs for the front, and 1½-inch logs for the door frame. To fit the pieces together snugly, place the 7-inch logs that form the sides of the cabin and the 1½-inch logs that make the door frame rounded sides up. Place the 9-inch logs that form the back and the 3- and 4-inch logs that form the front flat side up. Build the walls without frosting first to check log placement and order. Stack the walls 6 or 7 logs high. Use one or two 9-inch logs across top of front wall over the doorway. Once you're pleased, disassemble your log cabin; then reassemble it, piping icing between the logs to secure them (see illustration, opposite top).

Attach the roof, then front roof piece, piping icing on tops of all four walls.

To make the chimney, stack about six graham crackers, "gluing" them together with icing. Trim, if necessary, so they stand on a short edge under the roof on one side of cabin. Then stack three graham crackers together, fastening them with icing. Stand second stack on a short edge on top of

the first stack; use icing to attach to roof gable (see illustration, right bottom). Cover a small part of chimney with icing. Place nuts in icing immediately. Repeat, adding icing and nuts until chimney is covered.

Attach wheat wafers to roof for shingles, add breadsticks for roof peak.

Make as many windows as desired, decorating with icing. Attach breadsticks to porch corners and front roof corners. Score breadsticks to desired lengths with a knife; then snap to break.

Color some of the Royal Icing green and red. Use the colored icing to decorate the log cabin. Add a string of "lights" by piping red or green frosting along the edge of the house and adding small candies for lights. If desired, sift powdered sugar over roof or use some white icing to look like snow. Make icing icicles on the roof edges.

finishing touches

Add atmosphere and interest to your log cabin with these optional extras. Add as many as you wish.

Wagon Wheels: Pipe icing spokes and rims on purchased ginger snaps. Set next to cabin if desired.

Butter Churn: Attach a pretzel stick to a root beer candy with icing; add icing bands near top and bottom.

Fence: Break long pretzel sticks into desired lengths and assemble with icing.

fairy tale cottage

Prepare this dough twice—don't double it—or the dough will be too difficult to handle. Use leftovers to make cookie cutouts.

ingredients

½   cup butter, softened

½   cup shortening

1   cup sugar

1½   teaspoons ground ginger

1½   teaspoons ground allspice

1   teaspoon baking soda

½   teaspoon salt

1   egg

½   cup molasses

2   tablespoons lemon juice

3   cups all-purpose flour

1   cup whole wheat flour

    Special Sugar Cookie Cutouts (see recipe, page 143)

Bake: 10 minutes per batch Chill: 3 hours Oven: 375°F

1. In a large mixing bowl beat the butter and shortening with an electric mixer on medium to high speed for 30 seconds. Add the sugar, ginger, allspice, baking soda, and salt. Beat until combined, scraping sides of bowl occasionally. Add egg, molasses, and lemon juice and beat until combined. Beat in as much of the all-purpose flour as you can with the mixer. Using a wooden spoon, stir in any remaining all-purpose flour and whole wheat flour. Divide dough in half. Cover and chill about 3 hours or until dough is easy to handle.

2. Prepare Sugar Cookie dough according to step 1 of the recipe. Cover and chill about 2 hours or until dough is easy to handle.

3. Enlarge the patterns on pages 156-157 as directed. If desired, laminate pattern pieces to protect them. Using a floured rolling pin, roll some of the sugar cookie dough to ¼-inch thickness on the back of an ungreased 15×10×1-inch baking pan, following Special Cutting Instructions on page 150. Place pattern pieces 1 inch apart onto dough. Cut around patterns with a sharp knife. Remove excess dough (save for rerolling), leaving cutouts on pan. Bake in a 375° oven for 10 to 12 minutes or until edges are lightly browned. Leaving warm, baked cookies on pan, replace patterns and trim away excess dough. (The more exactly the pieces are cut, the easier the house will fit together.) Let cookies cool completely on pan; then transfer to wire racks.

fairy tale cottage decorating and assembly

ingredients

2   recipes Royal Icing (see recipe, page 40)

Paste food coloring

Waffle-creme cookies

Fruit-flavored gummy circle candies

Tiny candy-coated tart candies

Multicolored nonpareils

Graham cracker squares

Honey-roasted peanut halves

Frosted bite-size shredded wheat biscuits

Peppermint candy sticks

Gumdrops

Special Cutting Instructions: Cut one roof piece B from sugar cookie dough; turn pattern over to cut a second roof piece from the sugar cookie dough. Use sugar cookie dough to cut 2 roof pieces from pattern A.

Cut one end piece A from gingerbread dough for the middle of the house. For the tudor-style piece for the front of the house, cut pattern A on the dotted line. Roll out some gingerbread dough and some sugar cookie dough onto a lightly floured surface. Cut the rectangular piece of pattern A from gingerbread dough. Cut the triangular piece of the pattern from sugar cookie dough. Place the two pieces onto a greased cookie sheet with long edges touching. Roll lightly to seal. For beams, cut ¼-inch-wide strips from the gingerbread dough scraps. Place gingerbread strips on the sugar cookie dough end piece for tudor appearance (see illustration, opposite top). Using gingerbread dough, cut two sides from pattern A, two ends from pattern B, two sides from pattern B, and three chimney pieces from pattern B.

To decorate and assemble cottage: Assemble and display the cottage on waxed-paper-covered quilt batting set on a large tray or wooden cutting board. Pipe Royal Icing from a decorator bag fitted with small decorator tips, or spread icing to fasten pieces. Experiment to find the right amount of icing to use. If you apply too little icing, the pieces won't stay together, yet too much icing takes too long to dry. Let pieces stand about 1 hour or until icing is dry before continuing.

Prepare Royal Icing; tint as desired with paste food coloring. Using white icing, pipe outline of windows onto sides A and B. Pipe onto door and door trims onto tudor-style end piece A. Using yellow icing, fill in windows on house and door. Pipe on windowpanes. Fill in door with red icing. If desired, pipe Christmas light strings onto tudor beams or use icing to attach colored candies to look like a string of lights.

Separate waffle-creme cookies into two layers. Attach one cookie layer by each window for a shutter. Attach fruit-flavored circle candies for wreaths by door and tiny tart candy pieces above windows. Use green icing and a medium star tip to pipe a tree in one window; decorate with nonpareils. Using red icing and the small round tip, pipe a bow onto each shutter and wreath. For lights, use a small round tip to pipe small dabs of icing or add colored candy pieces to icing. Let icing dry thoroughly.

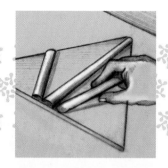

For porch, cut a graham cracker square in half lengthwise. Cut another square in half diagonally. Decorate a triangle with frosting and nonpareils. (Discard remaining triangle.) Assemble the porch roof; attach it to tudor-style end piece A. Let icing dry thoroughly before assembling the cottage.

Working on a surface covered with quilt batting, pipe icing through a star tip to assemble section A, joining sides and ends. Press pieces together. Assemble section B next to section A. Use a few dabs of icing to secure end sections of A and B together. Use glass measuring cups or heavy coffee mugs to hold pieces upright and steady until icing dries thoroughly.

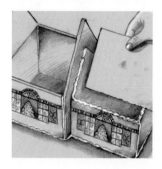

Using a star tip to pipe icing on edges of sides and end pieces of both house sections, press roof pieces into position, placing the notched ends of roof sections B at the outside edge (see illustration, right middle).

Join the three chimney pieces with icing, making one thicker piece; attach chimney to end of house section B, fitting chimney into notched area of roof. Spread one chimney area with icing. Place peanut halves into icing, allowing a little space between them so they look like stones (see illustration, right bottom). Repeat until chimney is covered with icing and nuts. Let dry.

Spread part of a roof section generously with icing. Press frosted wheat biscuits into the frosting, staggering the rows like shingles. Attach peppermint sticks to peaks of both roof sections. Use peppermint sticks and icing to support porch roof.

Touch a star tip to edge of roof. Squeeze the decorator bag gently; then pull down to taper the frosting to a point. Pull the tip away. Repeat around all roof edges to make icicles. Add other candy trims.

advent cookie tree

Count down to Christmas with this Advent tree hung with sugar-cookie cutouts artfully decorated with Royal Icing.

ingredients

Special Sugar Cookie
   Cutouts (see recipe,
   page 143)

Drinking straw

Royal Icing (see
   recipe, page 40)

Paste food coloring

Colored sugar and/or small
   silver or gold decorative
   candies

Thin satin ribbons

Prep: 35 minutes Chill: 1 hour Bake: 7 minutes per batch Oven: 375°F
Makes: 40 cookies

1. Prepare dough according to step 1 of the recipe. Divide the dough in half. Cover and chill dough about 1 hour or until dough is easy to handle.

2. On a lightly floured surface, roll half of the dough at a time to $\frac{1}{2}$-inch thickness. Using a variety of $2\frac{1}{2}$-inch Christmas cookie cutters, cut out dough. Place cutouts onto an ungreased cookie sheet.

3. Bake in a 375° oven for 7 to 8 minutes or until edges are firm and bottoms are very lightly browned. Immediately after baking, use a drinking straw to make a hole in each cookie top. Transfer cookies to a wire rack; cool.

4. Prepare Royal Icing and thin it with a little water just until it appears smooth when spread. Divide icing and tint desired colors with paste food coloring. Place some of each color into a decorating bag (no couplers or tips are needed). Spread a base of white colored icing over tops of cookies. (If desired, use an artist's paintbrush to apply the icing base.) Let icing base dry for 1 to 2 hours. Snip tips off decorating bags and pipe colored icing onto cookies. If desired, sprinkle colored sugar onto wet icing or press decorative candies into icing. Let cookies dry 1 to 2 hours. Carefully thread ribbons through holes in cookies and hang them on an ornament tree or branch. If desired, store decorated cookies in the freezer and take out one cookie each day during Advent to add to the tree or branch.

sugar cookie ornaments

Prep: 30 minutes Chill: 2 hours Bake: 8 minutes per batch

Oven: 375°F Makes: 40 cookie ornaments Assemble: 30 minutes

1. In a bowl stir together flour, baking powder, cardamom, and salt; set aside. In a saucepan combine butter, the 1 cup granulated sugar, and corn syrup. Cook and stir over medium heat until butter is melted and sugar is dissolved. Pour into a mixing bowl. Stir in vanilla. Cool 5 minutes. Add egg; mix well. Add flour mixture to egg mixture; mix well. Divide dough into four portions. Cover and chill at least 2 hours or overnight. For three-dimensional ornaments, on a lightly floured surface roll one portion of dough at a time to ⅛-inch thickness. Using a sharp knife, cookie cutters, or a fluted pastry wheel, cut dough into rounds, squares, diamonds, or heart shapes that are 3 to 4 inches wide. Make an even number of each shape, as you'll need to pair them together later.

2. Arrange the shapes on an ungreased cookie sheet. Cut half of the cookies in half from top to bottom, but do not separate the two halves. Using a straw, poke a hole off-center at the top of each whole cookie. Bake in a 375° oven for 8 to 10 minutes or until edges are light brown. Carefully cut halved cookies apart. Transfer to a wire rack, keeping cookie pairs together; cool. Prepare and tint Royal Icing with food coloring. Decorate cookies (wholes and halves) with icing. If desired, sprinkle wet icing with additional colored sugar, or add decorative candies. Let icing dry. To assemble, pipe icing onto cut edge of cookie half; attach cookie half to a whole cookie of the same size and shape. Let dry. Add icing and attach matching cookie half to the other side of the whole cookie. Let dry completely. Run a ribbon or yarn through the hole of each cookie; tie into a loop large enough for hanging on a tree.

ingredients

- 4   cups all-purpose flour
- 1   teaspoon baking powder
- ¾   teaspoon ground cardamom
- ½   teaspoon salt
- 1   cup butter
- 1   cup granulated sugar
- ⅔   cup light-colored corn syrup
- 1   tablespoon vanilla
- 1   beaten egg

    Drinking straw

    Royal Icing (see recipe, page 40)

    Paste food coloring

    Colored sugar, and/or decorative candies

    Narrow ribbon or yarn

pattern: gingerbread log cabin (pages 144-147)

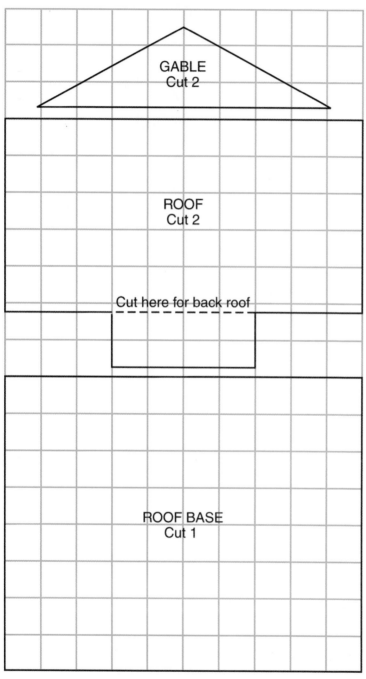

GABLE
Cut 2

ROOF
Cut 2

Cut here for back roof

ROOF BASE
Cut 1

1 SQUARE = 1 INCH

pattern: fairy tale cottage (pages 148-151)

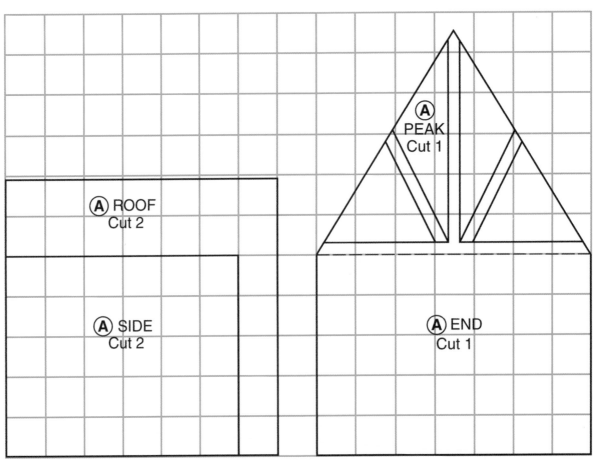

Ⓐ ROOF Cut 2

Ⓐ SIDE Cut 2

Ⓐ PEAK Cut 1

Ⓐ END Cut 1

1 SQUARE = 1 INCH

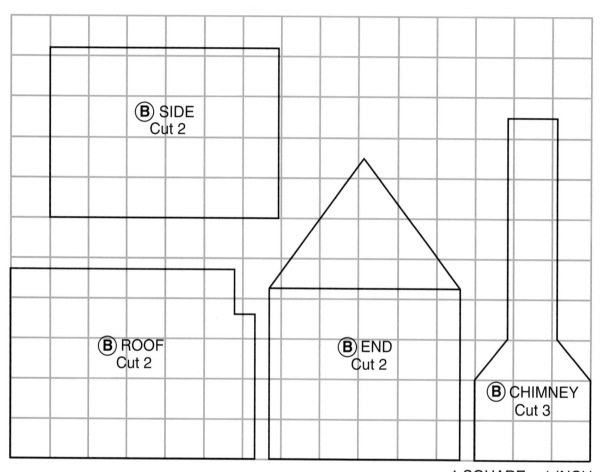

B SIDE
Cut 2

B ROOF
Cut 2

B END
Cut 2

B CHIMNEY
Cut 3

1 SQUARE = 1 INCH

metric information

The charts on this page provide a guide for converting measurements from the U.S. customary system, which is used throughout this book, to the metric system.

Product Differences

Most of the ingredients called for in the recipes in this book are available in most countries. However, some are known by different names. Here are some common American ingredients and their possible counterparts:

■ **All-purpose flour** is enriched, bleached or unbleached white household flour. When self-rising flour is used in place of all-purpose flour in a recipe that calls for leavening, omit the leavening agent (baking soda or baking powder) and salt.

■ **Baking soda** is bicarbonate of soda.

■ **Cornstarch** is cornflour.

■ **Golden raisins** are sultanas.

■ **Green, red, or yellow sweet peppers** are capsicums or bell peppers.

■ **Light-colored corn syrup** is golden syrup.

■ **Powdered sugar** is icing sugar.

■ **Sugar** (white) is granulated, fine granulated, or castor sugar.

■ **Vanilla** or vanilla extract is vanilla essence.

Volume and Weight

The United States traditionally uses cup measures for liquid and solid ingredients. The chart below shows the approximate imperial and metric equivalents. If you are accustomed to weighing solid ingredients, the following approximate equivalents will be helpful.

■ 1 cup butter, castor sugar, or rice = 8 ounces = 1/2 pound = 250 grams

■ 1 cup flour = 4 ounces = 1/4 pound = 125 grams

■ 1 cup icing sugar = 5 ounces = 150 grams

Canadian and U.S. volume for a cup measure is 8 fluid ounces (237 ml), but the standard metric equivalent is 250 ml.

1 British imperial cup is 10 fluid ounces.

In Australia, 1 tablespoon equals 20 ml, and there are 4 teaspoons in the Australian tablespoon.

Spoon measures are used for smaller amounts of ingredients. Although the size of the tablespoon varies slightly in different countries, for practical purposes and for recipes in this book, a straight substitution is all that's necessary. Measurements made using cups or spoons always should be level unless stated otherwise.

Common Weight Range Replacements

Imperial / U.S.	Metric
1/2 ounce	15 g
1 ounce	25 g or 30 g
4 ounces (1/4 pound)	115 g or 125 g
8 ounces (1/2 pound)	225 g or 250 g
16 ounces (1 pound)	450 g or 500 g
1 1/4 pounds	625 g
1 1/2 pounds	750 g
2 pounds or 2 1/4 pounds	1,000 g or 1 Kg

Oven Temperature Equivalents

Fahrenheit Setting	Celsius Setting*	Gas Setting
300°F	150°C	Gas Mark 2 (very low)
325°F	160°C	Gas Mark 3 (low)
350°F	180°C	Gas Mark 4 (moderate)
375°F	190°C	Gas Mark 5 (moderate)
400°F	200°C	Gas Mark 6 (hot)
425°F	220°C	Gas Mark 7 (hot)
450°F	230°C	Gas Mark 8 (very hot)
475°F	240°C	Gas Mark 9 (very hot)
500°F	260°C	Gas Mark 10 (extremely hot)
Broil	Broil	Grill

*Electric and gas ovens may be calibrated using Celsius. However, for an electric oven, increase Celsius setting 10 to 20 degrees when cooking above 160°C. For convection or forced air ovens (gas or electric), lower the temperature setting 25°F/10°C when cooking at all heat levels.

Baking Pan Sizes

Imperial / U.S.	Metric
9×1 1/2-inch round cake pan	22- or 23×4-cm (1.5 L)
9×1 1/2-inch pie plate	22- or 23×4-cm (1 L)
8×8×2-inch square cake pan	20×5-cm (2 L)
9×9×2-inch square cake pan	22- or 23×4.5-cm (2.5 L)
11×7×1 1/2-inch baking pan	28×17×4-cm (2 L)
2-quart rectangular baking pan	30×19×4.5-cm (3 L)
13×9×2-inch baking pan	34×22×4.5-cm (3.5 L)
15×10×1-inch jelly roll pan	40×25×2-cm
9×5×3-inch loaf pan	23×13×8-cm (2 L)
2-quart casserole	2 L

U.S. / Standard Metric Equivalents

1/8 teaspoon = 0.5 ml	
1/4 teaspoon = 1 ml	
1/2 teaspoon = 2 ml	
1 teaspoon = 5 ml	
1 tablespoon = 15 ml	
2 tablespoons = 25 ml	
1/4 cup = 2 fluid ounces = 50 ml	
1/3 cup = 3 fluid ounces = 75 ml	
1/2 cup = 4 fluid ounces = 125 ml	
2/3 cup = 5 fluid ounces = 150 ml	
3/4 cup = 6 fluid ounces = 175 ml	
1 cup = 8 fluid ounces = 250 ml	
2 cups = 1 pint = 500 ml	
1 quart = 1 litre	